Invisible Roots:

Overcoming the Complexities of Being A Woman in
Leadership

Sarah Andreas, Ph.D.

Published by WiseWood, LLC.

Strasburg, Ohio 44680 USA

Email: sarah@wisewoodllc.com • Subject Line: Invisible Roots

Visit our website:

www.wisewoodllc.com

WiseWood, LLC books are available for special promotions, premiums, or corporate training. For details contact WiseWood, LLC

Paperback ISBN: 978-0-9983303-6-5

Ebook: ISBN: 978-0-9983303-8-9

Library of Congress Control Number:2019909979

(WiseWood, LLC)

Andreas, Sarah

DEDICATION
    With all my heart to Dan and Marcus.

Acknowledgments

Throughout my journey of growth as a leader, an African proverb stands out. "If you want to go fast, go alone. If you want to go far, go together." It took me a long time to get comfortable asking others to journey with me, to speak into my life and to be a part of my adventures. For this book, I reached out to amazing people who I knew would give me feedback, ask questions, and help me make this book even better.

So, I offer a sincere thankyou to Diana and Tim Adour, Cassie Brown, Mike Davis, Cyndy Host, Diana Evans, and Cindy Ramey, and the women who became a part of my launch team. They all took the time to walk part of this journey with me. I will be forever grateful for their company, advice, and thoughts.

Contents

Chapter 1
My Wish for More Women in Leadership

"There's no point having wishes if you don't at least try to do them."
— Sally Nicholls, Author, Ways to Live Forever

I wished I could find a female role model who was successful in business and successful in her life. Have you ever made a wish? One you may not have said out loud, but it was a heartfelt, real, gut-wrenching wish for something to change, or to find what you needed?

Years ago, when I was struggling to see myself as a leader, a manager, a mother and wife, I made that wish.

I grew up in a small, rural, seasonal business. With my little bare feet covered with dust, I sold corn, green beans, and tomatoes at the end of my family's lane. It was during those long summer hours when I fell in love with business and selling. However, I struggled to move from a rural business and to feel that I could be successful in a more substantial business atmosphere. Looking around me, I saw successful people, and I was struggling to figure it out.

I wanted more. I wanted to *be* more, but I did not know any women who were successful who I could use as business models. I was determined to be successful in business, and later to be successful in leadership, so I decided to educate myself. I stopped looking for the best female role model and instead looked for the best role models. I found mentors, guides, and coaches to support my growth journey. Despite finding wonderful mentors, that wish to see *women* leaders was written on my heart. And no matter how much I tried to ignore it, it stuck.

Do you want to know the funny thing about a wish? It's about that wish I made to find a woman who was successful in business and in life. A couple months ago, when I was wrapping up my Ph.D. in Organizational Leadership, I had to do a reflection paper about my journey. Guess what I figured out? I had pushed that wish out into the world, a yearning for a role model, a woman who was successful in business and loved her life—and God pushed it back to me, saying, "Be her."

I was called. I did not realize it was my calling at the time. If I did, I am not sure I would have been brave enough to take the journey I have been on. Feeling a call to become different is scary. It requires putting yourself out in the world, putting yourself out where people can see your imperfections, where people can judge you, and where they can see your successes—and failures. The very act of wishing was my way of voicing my calling.

I went through a time where I did not know what I wanted to be when I grew up. I was in my late twenties, unsure and frustrated. There were no women who were active in my life and lived the kind of life I wanted to live, women who shared their love of business and their love of family. I wanted to be successful, but I was struggling to even know who I was as a woman and as a business leader.

Business today is often glossy, shiny, and all the cracks are hidden. The same is true of our lives. We share our high points, beauty and achievements on social media. This gloss on everything often portrays everything as perfect, and it sometimes seems as though everyone but us is super successful, and if we struggle with balancing our success in business with our family lives there is something wrong with us as women.

I started what I call my career as a business leader by working for a group of five Harley-Davidson dealerships in Ohio. I had jobs before where I was in charge, but it was working in the dealerships where I learned to lead. I was surrounded by motorcycles, riders, and an environment that was encouraging me to grow. This type of environment is unusual in business and almost unheard of in the Harley-Davidson dealerships. The owner's stance is they hire people from the neck up, meaning that their ability to lead others and manage the business is more important than gender.

I began as the e-commerce manager in charge of five people who were all older, had been there, and done that. While I was pretty knowledgeable about the technical side of e-commerce and business, I was not as effective as a leader and role model. I had not mastered the leadership skills truly needed to influence and lead others. I did have a willingness to learn and grow, which helped to offset my lack of knowledge and leadership skills. I was not aware of how to flex my communication techniques so my messages were received, and my team felt inspired. I had to grow these skills and build my internal leadership practice to become what I view as a successful woman in business. Even in a role where I was challenged and growing my skills as a leader, I was still struggling to know what and who I was really going to be when I became successful.

So I made a list of what I did not want to be, and it was a long list. Never, on my lists of things I do not want to do and my list of things I might want to do, did I write "I want to be an example of a successful businesswoman who loves business and her life; and to be an example of a successful woman in a leadership role." Never did I write, "I want to be an example." In fact, there were many times when I held myself back from being an example, because I did not want to be responsible for leading someone astray.

Until now, I have resisted my heart's urge to write a leadership development book for women. But I believe we need leaders—men and women—who are willing to step up and lead in an uncertain and changing world.

My internal battle, the call to focus on women in leadership, has been fierce. I have a son who I believe needs to learn the same content, lessons, and focus. I have spoken to women and men who believe there is a need for women to stand out as leaders. The tugging back and forth between my belief that this book should be written and my unwillingness to write it became a constant internal battle.

Because I was having such an internal battle, I did some soul searching. I felt the pull towards women in leadership, but my internal tension kept making me recoil. I had a list of great reasons for writing such a book, but I also had to understand why I was so determined *not* to write this book.

Part of increasing our self-awareness is the result of when we feel called to do something and realizing we are also very resistant to doing it. In this case, we need to dig deeper into why we feel both the call and the resistance.

As I reflected on why I was not willing to write a book about women and leadership, I kept bumping up against the way I was raised.

I did not know, years ago, that I would become the leader I am today. I had a dream of what my future life would look like, but I did not understand what leadership requires. I just knew that I wanted to be successful in business. I did not see the work, the changes, and the evolution I would need to endure to become the woman I am now.

Then I felt the call. It was time to step into the world, into the unknown, and become such a woman—to become the example I was looking for all those years ago.

I struggled with, and resisted, becoming comfortable being uncomfortable. I was scared. I cried. I struggled. I tried everything I could to stay where I was comfortable, to continue doing something I was good at, in a situation where people loved and supported me.

But as I looked around, I began to know, deep in my heart, that it was time.

When we get the "It is time" message, we must move. We don't want to look back and wish we had followed our hearts. If we don't move, we will see examples of other people taking action on our calling.

When I reflect back on when I started to feel the call, I must acknowledge that completing a Ph.D. was a delaying tactic. My Ph.D. helped me to grow and gain a deeper understanding of leadership development, but it was still a delaying tactic. I knew I was going to leave the career I loved, and I was trying to put it off long enough so I did not have to follow through with it.

I was the director of operations and training at the Harley-Davidson dealerships. It was challenging, and fun! I learned to ride a motorcycle. We had days when our management team took off and rode for a couple of hours in the middle of a workday. I made lifelong friends and wrote two *Women Who Ride* books because of the amazing women I have had the privilege to know. I had a fantastic team to work with every day. When I told Mike (my former leader) that in five years, I was leaving, he said "A lot could change in five years." I was hoping that my calling would change and I could remain the same.

Then I handed in my six months' notice in September of 2018. It was the longest, fastest six months of my life. I ended up working part-time for two additional months before becoming 100% self-employed. It was a leap of faith to step into my Creator's light and call other women to do the same.

When I looked around the smaller rural communities where I live, in churches and businesses, I still noticed that women are not showing up in leadership roles—women who are standing quietly and not owning the gifts our Creator has given them. Women who are wishing for something but not sure what they wish for. I felt called to stand up and talk about the lack of women who are visible in leadership roles. Women who are not dreaming and creating the lives they want to live. Women who don't even view themselves as a leader, even as they are leading the most important person in their life…themselves.

Throughout this book, I use the word visible. Visible, to me, means showing both our leadership gifts and our insecurities—and still shining. Show up! Be willing to follow, to lead, to speak up, to make tough choices, to show up as *a woman who takes action*. You are a leader who can be seen.

This is not meant to say, "look at me, I am great." Instead, it means "follow my example as a leader and go further." Marillyn Hewson, the Chairman, President and CEO of Lockheed Martin, the world's largest defense contractor, is an example of "follow my example as a leader and go further." In an interview with CBS This Morning, she attributed her success at Lockheed Martin to always saying yes to a promotion, even though her family had to move eight times during her career.[1] Saying yes is how she has received more and more opportunities to lead. She uses her example to encourage other women to do the same.

However, not every woman I speak to views themselves as a leader. Many women I have talked to don't hide their leadership gifts on purpose. They don't connect with the word leader; to them, it is a word reserved for high profile business and church leaders.

Nonetheless, women are being called to lead. The sad and scary thought for me is feeling the longing to lead, and then hiding—putting it off until there is a better time, a more inclusive, more open, and connected opportunity.

Other women need us to show them that leadership is not always high profile. To show them that we can be leaders as stay-at-home mothers and businesswomen. We can lead within our churches, and we bring unique gifts to the world through our leadership. We can lead by living lives full of love, joy and connections.

Generations of amazing women do not view

themselves as leaders, so they don't embody and share their gifts. These are women who are silent, and who were raised under the social constraints that women are "less than" and are not able to lead—women who wonder how they can make a difference in the world.

I was called to share my story, to offer my example of leadership, and to encourage you to share *your* story. Because in your story are the power of connection, community, and the power of the modeling a full, amazing life. I could not find that because other women around me did not view themselves as leaders, and they hid their gifts. We must be willing to be visible examples of women in leadership roles. If we don't, all the leadership role models will be men.

I met Diana Adour through her husband, Tim. Tim and I completed our Ph.D. journeys together. Diana is the Associate Pastor at the Church of the Revelation in The Bronx, New York. I knew of Diana through conversations with Tim about his wife. He would talk about her fierceness and what a great leader she is. What I first noticed about Diana is her way of being in a room. She has a natural glow that attracts people to her, and the way she stands invites people to be curious and wonder about her. When you see her, you would never guess that she grew up in a culture that genuinely believes women are owned. She was raised in India, in a culture where women "were to be seen, look good and serve the man, but not to voice an opinion" (those are her words). Throughout her educational journey, even in college, she was taught not to speak her thoughts and opinions out loud.

Diana shared the following story with me.

For years, there was the real me screaming inside to be heard. My voice was either rejected, considered petty, or even laughed at. I knew I had leadership qualities because they exhibited themselves in sports and academics, but I felt stifled.

Then I came to the United States and married an American. Tim, my husband, believed in me and saw my inner qualities, and when an opportunity arose for me to lead, he encouraged me to go for it. He took care of our two young kids, cooked and cleaned, did laundry, and dragged the kids to their school activities so that I could travel and be free to lead.

It took years before I was able to think for myself, have an opinion, and be confident enough to know someone valued my input. But my confidence grew, and so did the opportunities to lead. Today, I lead a large non-profit organization, and I love what I do. Interestingly, I work with and oversee many internationals, men and women. Some of them come from cultures just like mine, but the gift of leadership that was hidden for so many years is now evident, accepted, and followed, despite some who are still struggling with a female leader.

I must, however, be honest. When I return to my home culture, or other similar cultures, I find myself cowering once again because they still have a difficult time acknowledging that a woman can hold such status. Just recently, I was on an international trip leading dozens of people, but the leaders in that country could not acknowledge my leadership. They would not even look at me when I was introduced as the leader. Many of my team observed this berating and were angry, but I am now more confident in myself and my leadership, and it does not bother me like it once did. Nevertheless, I do hope that one day this will change, and others will learn that good leadership transcends culture, economic limitations, race and gender.

Diana embodies leadership. She is a shining example. Through the very act of showing up and standing in her own light as a visible leader, she shares an inner grace that comes from leading. This happens when we become confident as women and as leaders.

Being a visible leader does not mean you have to be the top-level CEO or a high-profile media sensation. It means you take ownership, and you embody your leadership, your calling. You own it. When you are given opportunities to lead, you take them. And when you are given, or make, chances to share, include, connect, and model leadership gifts, you do it. Marissa Mayer was the chief executive officer and president of Yahoo! Inc., and now is the cofounder of Lumi Labs. She said, "I always did something I was a little not ready to do. I think that's how you grow. When there is a moment of 'Wow, I'm not really sure I can do this,' and you push through those moments, that's when you have a breakthrough." [2]

My first lesson in taking the lead even when I was unsure about my abilities came through one of my first leadership roles. It was offered to me when I was nineteen years old. I was a crew member working at Taco Bell. I struggled with my internal dialogue, self-worth, and confidence back then. If you had asked me what was holding me back, I could not have told you what it was. I did not view myself as a leader or even imagine I could be a supervisor. The funny thing was, I was already fulfilling the role before I was offered the position, so there should not have been any hesitancy on my part.

The general manager pulled me into his office and told me about the leadership qualities he had observed in my performance. He told me I needed to stop worrying and overthinking it—just accept the job, and do what I did naturally.

This internal battle is one I have experienced over and over in my career, an invisible root that holds me down, coaxing me to be silent, obey, follow, and not to lead. That invisible root meant, to me, that I could do the work, but I could not be acknowledged as the leader, because owning my leadership gifts would be inappropriate.

I have finally reached the point where I can give myself the same talk my general manager gave me. To tell myself, "I am a professional. I have paid my dues. I know what I am talking about. I am good enough." I do not need an external source to confirm my abilities and push me away from that invisible belief about myself and women in leadership. I have learned to cheer for myself and for others who I try to inspire into standing in their own light. Becoming able to recognize that I was sabotaging myself and holding myself back from opportunities to lead because I was unsure, and allowing old stories and invisible roots to limit my future, was a long struggle. Have you held yourself back from taking the lead because of an old story?

When we allow old stories and self-doubt to influence our choices, when we choose to stand in the back, to be silent, invisible, to hold ourselves back and not stand in our light, we miss the opportunity to be a directional pointer for other emerging leaders. Instead, their path is guided by the current, visible leaders within our communities.

If you feel the call, if you wish for more women to be visible in leadership, then *you* must become the directional marker lights, so the women who are coming after you can follow.

When I put my stake in the sand and said, "I am going to do this. I am going to be a vulnerable, visible, public example of a successful woman in leadership," I found the woman I was searching for when I needed such a model. However, this was the surprising part; she was not just one woman.

I looked around, and I found women who were loving their lives, their families, their kids. Women who loved their careers and were passionate about their goals. Women who lived with energy, courage, and generosity. Women who were tough and kind. I found them all because I was looking through a different lens, a lens created by years of intentional leadership development. The young women who are actively seeking female role models may not have the leadership development background to find you when you are hiding. We need to take every opportunity we can to find, create, and be directional markers on their life maps.

I am not 100% sure how the connection works, but I am sure the very act of *becoming* allows us to see the world differently. It enables us to find what we were looking for because we find it in ourselves first.

We must be willing to do the work. We must be willing to put ourselves out there—to be brave, to stand in the Creator's light instead of trying to hide it because we don't want others to be uncomfortable and because we don't want to be uncomfortable. We have to learn to embrace being uncomfortable, and to become comfortable with being uncomfortable.

When we are called to be visible leaders, it is because it is our calling to support and challenge others to live their callings too. We are called to become more than what we saw in ourselves before, to become leaders who the next generations can see and model themselves after.

Every day, we touch people's lives and their hearts. We influence them, and that is what leadership is all about. Our influence can become a directional sign in other people's journeys, but we are touching them. Leadership does not just happen in business or in churches. It happens in everyday life. It happens in small conversations, and in moments in time when we touch someone's life without even being aware that we have made a difference.

I often share that my progression into leadership and

my passion for leadership development is a God thing. As I was looking for female role models, I was blessed with four men in my life who were lighted directional markers on my life map. The first one was a teacher, Mr. Brehul, who encouraged me to stay in high school when I would otherwise have dropped out. Tom LaRochelle shared that he saw something great in me and suggested I should pay attention to and track my professional development. My husband Dan, who believes in me, models patience, offers his calm acceptance and lives in the current moment. And my most recent mentor and leader is Mike Davis. I think God knows I can be hard, stubborn, and challenging to deal with, so he presented me with Mike. Mike had no real reason to take an interest in helping me to grow and become a leader, but he has invested years of his life in helping me to become aware, challenging me to become more, and building a bridge which has allowed us to have hard conversations.

It is funny how the influence of these men has helped me to become more aware of the need to be a female role model for leadership. After deeper reflection, I don't know if a female leader could have helped me to break through my most significant barrier, the deeply-held belief that women always need to be subservient to men. Each of these men, in their unique ways, challenged me to become a strong, assertive, confident leader. They modeled their leadership strengths so I could find mine.

Over the past ten years, I have found women I have purposefully invited into my sphere of influence, women who have helped me understand and deal with the challenges I have faced as a woman, wife, mother, and leader.

Franscene Davis once told me about the seasons in our lives. I was struggling with what I wanted to be able to do professionally, and my son (who I adore) was very young at the time. In a passing conversation, she said, "Sarah, there are seasons in each of our lives. You just have to be able to identify the season." I will always be grateful for those words. Learning that motherhood with a small child is only a short season in our lives, I found in that season I could continue to prepare myself as a leader and be Marcus's mom at the same time. Learning to embrace both the journey and the season helped me to accept the pull I felt to push hard in my career and to stay close to my family. I put off making a career change that would require me to do extensive traveling so I could be home almost every evening with Dan and Marcus. I am so happy I made that choice. I don't feel cheated at all in my career; in fact, the time I spent as Marcus's mom allowed me to grow into becoming the leader I wanted to find all those years ago. Being aware of the seasons in my life allows me to embrace each season as it happens while preparing for the next.

Other women in my life include Dr. Alisha Crumpton, my dissertation chairperson, Dr. Marj Carlson Hurst, Cyndy, Diana, and Cindy from my MBA program. They all model what I consider to be feminine leadership with their ability to connect, share their hearts of gold, and their "take no prisoners, no excuses" attitude—a leadership style I am comfortable modeling myself. They have taught me to connect, to build relationships, to care for others, and to hold a standard for greatness.

In their own ways, each of these women has taught me a different aspect of how to become the leader I wanted to be, and how to live a life full of connections, love, abundance, courage, discipline, energy, grit, compassion, and success. They also taught me the importance of being visible.

As I prepared for the next season I am entering, I wrote several books, earned a master's degree at Malone University in Canton, Ohio and a Ph.D. in Organizational Leadership from Johnson University in Knoxville, Tennessee.

I have been delighted to see Marcus change from a struggling kid in school to a confident young man who has graduated from high school and is pursuing a career in computer technology. He is a third-degree black belt, and teaches five- to twelve-year-olds Tae Kwon Do one night a week as a master instructor. He is finding his own success, his own way of leading in the world. I am so honored I have been able to be a part of his life growing up. I would have missed so many of these moments if I had been traveling.

There is a Buddhists saying, "When the student is ready, the teacher will appear." I think our Creator puts wise leaders in our lives at just the moment we need to hear something. If we are listening, we will hear the message.

Each phase of our lives is precious, and we need to embrace our life journey. However, many women I have talked with have lost their abilities to dream, to have a vision for their future, and to take action towards progressing on their journey. Others have the ability but are no longer willing to take the chance and push themselves out of their comfort zone.

As each opportunity to learn, listen, grow and apply (or do) is presented to us, we have two choices. We can change, grow, and adapt, or we can pretend we don't feel the call.

We cannot force others to grow and develop. We can only influence their growth. We can understand the complexities of their development, offer our support, and challenge them to embrace their opportunities.

The same is also true for us. We can take courage and live our lives to the fullest. We can be a leader who understands the journey is essential and how we walk it is our example to those who follow.

Responding to the call for more women to be a light shining on the path of future leaders is essential. As leaders, women bring gifts of inclusion, connection, and encouragement. However, when women who are emerging into their leadership look around for leaders to model themselves after and only find men as role models, we may ignore some of the gifts our Creator has given us as a part of our innate leadership style because they don't match those of our mentors. And if we don't have role models who are from different genders, races, and ways of being in the world, we miss out of the true beauty we can bring as leaders.

Take A Deep Breath and Reflect

What have you wished for? What has been on your heart and mind that you are trying to ignore? Chances are that is your calling, the role you are being called to step into. Before I was even aware, I was called. I was drawn to stand, to show up, to let my light shine. I had that wish.

The moment when you realize you have been called you have two choices: Close your heart, mind, and spirit off; or embrace the scary uncertainty, and stand in your light. You get to choose, and your choices will impact people in ways you may never know. If you have denied your calling because you were scared, unsure, and unconfident, some individuals who are following you will not be pushed further because they stood in your light. If you embrace your calling, then you will impact others who, because you lived your calling to the fullest, can go farther and do more because of your influence.

Take Action

Start a reflection notebook. Buy one that is special, beautiful, charming, or makes you smile. You can choose to use the *Invisible Roots Reflection Journal.* Be excited about writing in it and dreaming about your future. Dreams are a great place to start your vision of your future self, even if you are not 100% sure what you are being called to do or be. Sometimes it helps to make lists of what you are not going to *do* or *be* to open your eyes to the unique gifts you have.

If you already know what you are called to be or do take a moment to celebrate that calling. Then, write down what your calling is in your reflection notebook. Next, take a deep breath and make a commitment to the next step in your journey. Write your next steps in your reflection notebook.

Chapter 2
Past Influences and Hijacks

"Successful people maintain a positive focus in life no matter what is going on around them. They stay focused on their past successes rather than their past failures, and on the next action steps they need to take to get them closer to the fulfillment of their goals rather than all the other distractions that life presents to them." - Jack Canfield, American author

I believe leadership is a significant topic for women to discuss and work towards developing. For years the examples of leaders were all male in almost every industry. Young women growing up did not see women who were actively leading. Even today, when we as women have more rights in America than at any other time, we still do not have even close to an equal number of women who are visibly leading.

Practicing leadership is something each of us can do within our own lives. Finding our dreams, putting a plan together and carving the path we take towards fulfilling our dreams paves the way for others. When leadership is effective something magical happens, and it becomes more than just basic math. Leaders who practice leadership within themselves and for others become inclusive, inviting and inspire the same in the people who interact with them.

I believe one of the hardest leadership lessons that I had to learn was how to be a great follower of myself. I was pretty good at following others, but I did not have a dream or vision of who I wanted to be and how I wanted to show up in the world. I was born a leader, one who needed a lot of polishing, but a leader nonetheless. Even feeling that I was born to lead did not empower me to lead myself. Looking back, I can see that a lot of my struggles as I was growing up came from a desire to lead, but at that time I lived in an environment that did not support women as leaders. I never learned to feel confident about leading myself, so I struggled to lead others effectively.

I grew up in an environment where women were taught to be subservient—to be silent, to accept the decisions made by men—and not be action-oriented and strong-minded. My parents were young; my mom was 16, and my dad was 17 when they had me. They were just trying to survive as a young, unsupported couple with a family of four children to raise and feed. They found solace in their faith and church. So, I grew up in a nondenominational Church of God where the expectation for young women was that they would grow up, get married, obey their husband, raise babies, and nothing more.

Standing in the basement hallway of the church when I was twelve, I thought I was being called to be a preacher. Because of the beliefs of that church, as I perceived them, I felt women were less important and less worthy than men. Women were lucky if they could lead Sunday school; they were not allowed to lead a church.

That was when the seed was planted in my heart.

I began to consider that maybe God had more in store for me, but I would have to leave a place of comfort to recognize and develop my potential. I found that I questioned a God who, in my twelve-year-old mind, created me in His image and then made me feel I was less than males, and not as capable as males because of my gender.

I left the church feeling angry at men, God, and women who allowed themselves to be treated in that manner. Years later, as I studied leadership, I learned to separate God from the church and from the belief that women were somehow inferior to men.

Eventually, I was able to find love for the church where I grew up. While their faith and beliefs are right for them, those beliefs were not right for me. I had to learn to love and respect their views, even though I do not agree with them, so I could love and respect that I was called to be different. Even though I learned to love them, it did not erase my internal story that a follower is subservient to the leader and women could not lead. Because of this deeply rooted belief that women could not lead, and because of my firm (ok, maybe vehement) rejection of that belief, I had to learn to be humble.

I had to learn to be a great follower—and that following did not lessen my ability to lead. I had to learn to care for and lead myself in a full leadership practice. I had to learn that taking care of others, building connections, and finding ways to include people did not reduce my ability to lead—that I could care about and connect with people while still leading and creating the life I wanted.

What I discovered on my journey is that when a leader has a vision that is bigger than themselves, and they share that vision, it is an invitation for others to join them. Supporting another leader's vision is not about being subservient, it is about supporting the vision, and gender is unimportant for fulfilling that purpose.

So, when I think about the type of leadership I want to practice, it is inclusive leadership, not the subservient follower type. Even great leaders follow someone or something. They follow a calling towards a higher purpose, they follow other great leaders who have gone before them, or they follow their Creator.

Learning to follow and to be a great follower, I believe, allows me to lead more effectively. If I had held on to my past experiences, and the emotions and feelings I had, I would have become bitter and unwilling to follow any male role model, because that would have required me to follow. I could have held on to the experiences, emotions, and feelings I experienced as a young woman growing up in that environment, or I could choose to let it go. I decided to let it go.

Each of us, no matter where we are on our journey, are leading in some way. This lesson is one I have shared before, and I wrote about it in my first book for emerging leaders.[1]

I took part in a leadership development program years ago, and one of the classes was on diversity and inclusion. The instructor asked our class to stretch a piece of green tape across the floor and line up on it. He then gave us instructions to take a step forward if we took a vacation when we were a kid, then take a step back if we received free lunches. As we took our steps, the group began to separate. Some participants moved far into the front, and others moved slightly to the front or behind the green tape. Then there were three of us who were in the far back. I will never forget standing there and thinking, "This is where I started—all the way back here."

When the instructor asked if we had any thoughts or observations I waited for about three seconds, and then I raised my hand. I remarked that the exercise was an excellent example of where each of us had started, but it did not show all the time, effort and work I had put into becoming able to be in the room with the other leaders.

So the instructor came back to me and said, "I understand. Let me walk with you to the front of the room."

So I moved to the front of the room and was facing the wall. He asked, "What do you see?"

I replied, "I see my future and all the potential and opportunities I still have."

"What don't you see?" he asked. I was not sure what he was asking, so he had me turn around. And as I turned around, I saw all the people who were behind me, struggling to improve their leadership, striving to become more successful, to become better fathers, mothers, human beings—and I had walked by them all. I had not even noticed them or their struggles.

This is the lesson I learned from that activity. Each of us, on our journey, is ahead of someone else. And each of us can stand where we are, take a deep breath, and find the courage to go back and walk beside someone who is a couple of steps behind us, to help them move past the obstacles we moved passed, and to encourage them on their journey.

I took that class in 2012 but was not until 2017 when the lesson really bloomed in my awareness. The instructor pointed out that it is not just the experience, but the preparation, understanding, and ability to make meaning from our experiences helps leaders to develop leadership skills. Just having an experience is not crucial; we can *learn from our experiences*, and that is crucial.

This lesson has become part of my foundation for encouraging you to be a visible woman in a leadership role.

Some young women want to be effective leaders, and being willing to share your gifts with them is an essential piece of their growth. Be prepared to talk with them about their experiences, and how experiences shape us as women and as leaders. Help them learn to make meaning of their experiences in a way that frees them. It is essential.

The call to leadership requires you to be committed to something bigger than yourself, be it a higher purpose, a way to answer a need, or by creating an opportunity that is bigger than you can do on your own. This type of leadership requires a more in-depth, more profound development than just learning about leadership and taking action. It truly is about becoming a leader. To begin such a journey, I invite you on a journey of self-discovery in which you are supported and challenged in developing your leadership skills.

Take A Deep Breath and Reflect

Looking back on your life, there may be times when you have experienced something similar to what I went through. Were you were made to feel less than others by a person, church, or business group? Perhaps you also walked past individuals who were struggling on your way to your bright, prosperous future. Maybe you had experienced but did not learn from them, or you may not even have been aware of the experience. You just went through it and moved on without giving it any thought. Or perhaps you are still holding on to the feelings from your past experiences.

I clearly remember the feelings I had when I was participating in that class. I was angry. I felt belittled and very vulnerable standing in the back of the room, standing there where everyone could see where I had started in my life. I had gone out of my way to leave that version of myself in the past.

I could easily have held on to those feelings and missed the critical lesson the instructor taught me towards the end of class. If so, I would have missed the fact that I had walked past people who I could have helped. I may have missed the calling to help others develop their leadership skills so they can advance in their lives and careers, and go even further than I have gone in my career. The same experience can be viewed from multiple perspectives.

The perspective we choose to make our truth from affects us, whether we are aware of it or not.

Take Action

In your reflection journal, answer the following questions. First, what feelings and emotions from your past are you holding on to? Can you list them?

Can you start to accept them for what they are—something

that was given to you—and can you let them go?

If you are holding on to feelings and emotions from your past experiences but did not take the time to learn the lesson from them, I can guarantee that they are holding you back from achieving your true potential as a leader. These feelings don't have to be negative; they could be positive, even experiences of success, feelings of "I have achieved and arrived." They could be experiences of failure or fear, too.

I invite you to take a couple of minutes and just reflect on any experiences you may be holding on to that are no longer serving you—any feelings, emotions, or thoughts that allow you to justify hiding your gift for leadership.

Invisible Roots

Chapter 3
Leadership Gifts

"It is a holy blessing to be born with the exquisite qualities of a daughter of God... Never belittle the gifts God has given to you. Develop the divinity that is within you." - Margaret D. Nadauld

There is still a debate about whether leaders are born or made. I think it is a little of both.

If someone is a natural (born) leader but doesn't sharpen their natural talent or find the place where they are meant to lead, they will wither and not reach their full potential. Leaders who are developed find their passion and strive to become a person of influence, to see their vision of what could be become a reality. No matter which type of leader you are, you need to develop your leadership skills to reach your full potential. This type of growth involves work in both intrapersonal (inside yourself) and interpersonal (between you and other people) development. Both intrapersonal and interpersonal development requires the abilities to recognize, adapt and change your past stories, ways of being, and core beliefs, as well as mastering core leader and leadership skills. Learning to grow in two directions (intrapersonally and interpersonally) at the same time can be challenging.

You may notice that I sometimes refer to leader development and leadership development as two different things. In my mind, I separate them into intrapersonal and interpersonal development. Being a leader is a quality inside a person, the result of their intrapersonal development. Leadership is your effect on other people, called relational or interpersonal development. I often envision the yin and yang symbols, which are two separate yet intrinsically connected parts of a whole. Developing one without the other is not as effective. A leader is a whole person, we are not just one-dimensional, and this is where the real challenge of leader and leadership development begins. Developing a leader, or as a leader, is more than just learning skills; it is genuinely about internal growth.

Intrapersonal development is focused on you. You can grow, adapt, and change. It includes your ability to build and maintain an internal leadership practice, and learning to be connected within yourself. Understanding your dreams, talents, and gifts is part of an internal leadership practice, as is the ability to become and embrace your authentic self.

We need to become the leaders we are meant to be, which means we need to learn to be ourselves—with more skill. [1] This requires more than just the scaffolding of leadership skillsets, such as communication, connection, teamwork, etc. It requires more profound internal skills and abilities to develop an internal leadership practice that allows each of us to take a more in-depth look at ourselves, accepting whatever we perceive to be positive or negative, and loving ourselves because of them. This makes it essential to develop the ability to think about and assess ourselves, to have reflective conversations, and to be in community with people who will challenge us to become what our Creator has called us to be.

Interpersonal development is a process based on your ability to grow, adapt, and change in relation to another person or a group of people. It is leadership within a community, whether it's your town council or a group of like-minded individuals who share a common interest or passion. Also, interpersonal development enhances being a leader, being a follower, and our awareness that we affect more than ourselves. Our leadership, or lack of leadership, affects us, our communities, our futures, and the futures of those who will be coming within our sphere of influence.

I often say that we are the marker on someone else's life map. Our decision to lead and stand in our own light may have ripple effects that continue to flow long after we are no longer here.

We need both intrapersonal and interpersonal

development to become effective leaders. Often it is tempting to ignore the internal work we need to do in favor of the interpersonal work because the interpersonal work is visible to others, and in some ways it's easier to accomplish. Other people instantly recognize when we become better communicators, or we become more inclusive, and we get positive feedback from our efforts.

On the other hand, our internal leadership practice is not always visible to other people. They cannot easily see that we have been thinking about our own experiences, learning from them, and learning to accept ourselves, as we continue to develop our ability to lead effectively.

Our intrapersonal development is what we are going to focus on throughout this book. It will develop your ability to identify, understand and embrace your gifts—all of them—even the ones you might view as weaknesses. And this book will help you to develop an internal leadership practice, show you how to celebrate the leader you are right now, and begin the dream for the leader you are meant to become.

If, as leaders, we don't do this internal work, we miss our best opportunity to truly become whole. It is through this process of understanding, loving, and having compassion for ourselves we can extend those feelings to others.

In their book, *Athena Doctrine: How Women (and the Men Who Think Like Them) Will Rule the Future*, authors John

Gerzema and Michael D'Antonio talk about the skills people associate with masculine, feminine, and neutral leadership attributes. For me, two of the most exciting things are that the attributes people associate with leadership can be found in both men and women, and the perceptions of leadership attributes were consistent across countries. The authors did research to understand people's perceptions of leadership qualities, and they found that the qualities that were seen as feminine leadership attributes were the ones that people believed would make the world a better place. These leadership attributes are inclusion, sharing credit, intuition, collaboration, and being able to consider multiple views of a situation.

As I was reading the book, I thought that many of these feminine attributes are gifts we women may possess naturally. Gifts such as being trustworthy, helpful, dependable, adaptable, creative, sincere, cooperative, friendly, empathetic, encouraging, patient, affectionate and understanding were all words that, if I did not hide them, I could claim as my own.

When I started on my leadership journey, I buried these gifts in favor of a leadership style that reflected what I perceived as a stronger, more professional leadership style. Some of these masculine attributes, such as being strong, ambitious, focused, brave, daring, assertive, confident, and independent helped me to become courageous enough to embrace the feminine attributes. I believe they helped me to become a better version of myself, and they are still appealing to me.

41

However, it was when I learned to embrace my whole self and not hide the attributes I used to associate with being "soft," and when I learned to embrace all my characteristics, all my qualities, that I began to find a more genuine, more authentic kind of leadership. Using both my masculine and feminine attributes has helped me to become the leader I am today.

Mary Barra, CEO of GM, is an example of using the feminine leadership gifts of inclusiveness, listening, and approachability. She has created an environment where anyone can share their opinions. She then uses the masculine leadership gift of decisiveness. She was quoted in the LA Times. "At the end of the day, the decision has to be made. If we don't have complete unanimity, I have no qualms about making it." [1] Mary demonstrates that as women we can use all of our gifts to make our leadership effective.

If we are going to be visible female leaders, we need to do the internal work which allows us to be authentically whole. We need to bring all of our gifts, selves, and abilities to how we lead and influence others. This is how our real abilities as leaders can shine.

Take A Deep Breath and Reflect

This journey into becoming a woman who is visible and confident in her leadership, a woman who can be vulnerable and strong at the same time, who can hold opposing views and opinions without feeling threatened and being defensive is a challenging task, and it takes courage.

It takes a lot of courage to stand. When I make the statement about standing, I think of a lighthouse at the edge of a cliff. It shines light in the middle of storms. It is a directional marker for ships, just as we are directional markers for other emerging leaders.

We can answer the calling from our wish for more women in leadership roles, and we can be examples of women who embrace the gifts which make us the leaders we are called to be. We need to start with ourselves. We need to do the hard, internal work that forces us to look at our assumptions and our experiences. We need to take a hard look at the stories we have been telling ourselves, and decide whether they are serving our higher purpose or allowing us to hide, and feel justified in not being visible because we tell ourselves, "I am just a..."—you fill in the blank. What are your "I am just a…" statements? Are they helping you to lead visibly, or are they holding you back? How are they helping or holding you back?

Take Action

Identifying and understanding your gifts is essential to being able to become a visible leader. Choose five of the most supportive people in your life and ask them what gifts you have as a leader.

There are many assessments available to help you gain a better understanding of yourself and your gifts. I like the DiSC assessment to find out communication and behavior tendencies. Take the personality test at 16personalities.com *(it is free, as of 9/27/19),* and understand more about yourself as an individual. Then reflect on what you learn about yourself and your gifts in your reflection journal.

Also, identify one person who you see as having leadership potential and tell them which leadership gifts and abilities you think they have. Start a conversation and a relationship with them.

Chapter 4
The Stories We Tell Ourselves

"The great courageous act that we must all do is to have the courage to step out of our history and past so that we can live our dreams." — Oprah Winfrey

The internal stories we tell ourselves become a filter for our future thoughts, explanations of experiences, and ways of showing up in the world. The internal stories are how we make sense or meaning out of experiences and situations. Some authors refer to this process as a lens, or frames of references which we view our experiences through. I refer to it as the internal stories we tell ourselves and believe to be true.

We all see the world and interpret our current situation and experiences based on our past experiences. We build internal stories that are part of our assumptions and guiding tendencies. Internal stories become a habit we use to make meaning of each experience we have. These internal stories also hold our feelings, attitudes, and beliefs. Our stories become so embedded in us, they become habits and actions which automate our reactions and responses without us actively thinking about them. We can unconsciously make decisions and act without conscious thought, and it starts a loop. We had a reason or past experience that caused us to form the first internal story, and then it becomes an internal map of reality we use in guiding our life. These internal stories become so embedded that it can be difficult for us even to consider a different way of thinking.

The other factor that makes the stories we tell ourselves complicated is the way our minds develop. Kegan's theory of adult development explains how people change and grow cognitively throughout their lives. How we make meaning out of our experiences is a complicated process that we go through when we are having an experience. Making sense of what happened can occur without a conscious thought from us; we take the experience, filter the experience through the stories we tell ourselves, and assign meaning to the experience based on an old story.

For example, if you worked for a tyrant of a manager, and every time you spoke up in a meeting the manager looked at you, berated you, then gave you the silent treatment, you made meaning of that experience. As a result, you have a story about speaking up in a meeting. Those past experiences, and how you interpreted those experiences, can impact on your ability to speak up in a meeting. If you allowed that experience to unconsciously become the story you tell yourself, such as thinking you don't have useful input to offer or managers do not like people speaking up, even when you move to a new company and work for a manager who appreciates your unique views, that old story would still play through your subconscious. So now, when you are in a meeting, and your manager is silent, you may interpret that silence as disapproval and react accordingly.

The challenge is to identify that the story may not be accurate, and make a new meaning of the new manager's silence. Taking the time to talk to your manager and ask the question about their silence seems easy to do, but in fact, it takes courage. It takes courage because you have a negative story running through your head created by your past experiences. If you take a deep breath and ask the question, you may find that your new manager was silent because you were doing a great job and they are glad you are on their team. However, you cannot even get to this stage if you cannot recognize the stories you are telling yourself.

Each level of our cognitive development filters and builds meaning differently. Our minds are amazing, and I stand in awe of the power we hold within ourselves. The way we make meaning changes as we develop our cognitive abilities. There are three levels of adult cognitive meaning-making which are a part of adult development theory, and these three levels can influence how we lead.[2] These levels do not align with physical age. Instead, they develop as we are on our journey and from exposure to other ways of stretching our internal stories.

These three levels of adult cognitive meaning-making are the socialized, the self-authored, and the self-transforming mind. Each of these minds has profoundly different ways of making meaning and operating within the world. Each mind has a different type of filter through which we perceive and interpret our experiences, and each has inherent strengths and weaknesses. While it may be tempting to view one mind as more significant than the others, Berger believes that early mindsets are a fundamental point on a developmental path and should not be considered as a personality flaw to be corrected. So be nice to yourself as you grow and stretch your way of thinking. Each of us must grow through each phase. We often repeat phases, and we can find ourselves in-between two stages. No matter which mindset we have at any particular time in our lives, we can still lead in our own way and make a positive impact on the lives of others.

Socialized mindset

Individuals with a socialized mindset are mainly influenced and shaped by their personal and social environment. When we operate using our socialized mindset, we put our own desires to the side and align ourselves with the norms and standards of our environment and the individuals who are around us. We adopt the ideas or emotions of others who seem to align with our personal views. In essence, we create a filter that asks, when decisions are required, "What would person X or Y do?" and our choices are based on the external influence. If we look up to successful people or people who are influential for their positive impact, such as Oprah or Mother Teresa, we will use the behaviors and decisions they have modeled. If we are using role models who are not positive, then our choices and decisions are riskier.

This socialized mindset is influential in creating relationships and harmony within our social environment. However, there is a drawback. The socialized mindset strongly affects how we filter information and experiences. Because the socialized mind often wants harmony within our environment, there is a tendency toward groupthink, in which we will not share our ideas about something not working to avoid being perceived as a non-team player.

Pause: Do you find yourself wondering what someone else would do in your situation, or do you press forward? Are you willing to share your opinion even when it does not match the opinion of people you are talking with? If you find yourself holding back, you may be in a socialized mindset. You may want to think about how you can share your thoughts.

Self-authored mindset

As we begin to mature in our mindset, there is a movement from a socialized mindset toward a self-authored mindset. The self-authored mind builds on the socialized mind, but now we can include ourselves in the equation when making decisions. With this mindset we can examine the rules, opinions, and expectations from the most important ideologies, institutions, or people in our lives and mediate between differing views using our own internal self-governing system. We begin to be able to look objectively at situations we are involved with, instead of relying on someone else's opinion.

When we have a self-authored mindset, we gain the abilities to reflect on, question, and accept or deny other points of view or doctrines instead of following without thought. We learn to pause and ask ourselves, "What would I do?" instead of "What would Oprah do?" and be comfortable with our decision-making process. As we learn to master this, there is a transition toward a self-transforming mindset.

Pause: Are you able to look objectively at yourself within a situation? Can you separate yourself from the emotions, feelings, and outcomes to generate a broader view of what you are experiencing?

Self-transforming mindset

A self-transforming mind builds on the self-authored mind. A self-transforming mind can create inclusion and find likenesses where once there were only differences. This mindset is advanced, and only about 1% of the population shows signs of it.

Within this mindset, we are more aware that our internal filtering system could be flawed, and an examination of the filter is started by stepping back, instead of continuing to look at the world through an unexamined filter.

A self-transforming mind looks for and invites different voices and opinions, purposely finding diversity in thought, not just views agreeing with their current internal stories. This is where I believe the best leadership and leader mastery resides. As we develop this mindset we learn to cooperate with a rival or someone who has an exceptionally different point of view, because we will learn something new and it will challenge the way we currently understand the world.

No matter which mindset is the primary one we use, as humans, we use our sensors, such as our abilities of touching, seeing, and hearing, to filter information. Before collected information goes to our brain for processing, we run it through a filter of some type. All these mindsets have filters that prevents information from not being looked or from passing through to conscious awareness. This filter automatically places a priority on the information and experiences we have, and if the information is essential to our plan, it gets passed to the brain. If the information has not been sought and does not seem to have relevance to the plan, it has a much harder time getting through our filters.

Our automatic filters can become counterproductive when the internal stories we tell ourselves are flawed or outdated.

Each of our mindsets has different filters and internal stories influencing how we interpret experiences, process information, and view opportunities and challenges, as we are learning to lead in a more complex world.

Today, leadership requires more than just a set of skills. Leadership requires the ability to see and understand many situations in different contexts. Leaders need to be able to pull from both their own experiences and thoughts and the thoughts and experiences of others. The ability to view situations with less subjective and more objective viewpoints allows us to detach ourselves from the situation.

We need to be able to look at, engage, respond and reflect on any situation. Whether it is a story we created, a word someone else assigned to us and we took ownership of it, or the way something made us feel, any or all of these things have become the filters we use to make judgments about what we can and cannot accomplish.

For example: if, when you were a child, your parents were loving and supportive, and they labeled you as gifted, gifted becomes a word you filter through, sometimes unconsciously, when making decisions. You may think, "Being labeled as gifted is not bad. I would have loved to have been told I was gifted." Yet even labels, filters, and positive stories can create a prison. What does thinking of yourself as gifted keep you from doing? Does it keep you from trying things you may not be good at? Does it keep you from new experiences because your filter decides, on an unconscious level, that the experience may not align with the concept of your gift? If you are a gifted storyteller, does it mean you cannot become a teacher, an administrator, a salesperson, or a corporate trainer? Do you see the trap?

If you grew up in an unsupportive family, you could

have the same struggles with your filters. For example, if your parents were unhappy with a decision you made and they yelled at you, you may have built a belief that yelling is an appropriate way to communicate disagreement. Or, you may have grown up in a culture with a profound dislike for people who are different. Or you may have never been exposed to people who have disabilities. All of these can affect your effectiveness as a leader and your leadership methods.

Maybe the story is a label you gave yourself as you have been promoted and advanced in your career. If you labeled yourself as successful. It can be easy to think of a positive label within our internal stories as essential. But what does it hold you back from doing? Does the success story stop you from spending time with your family and friends? Has it caused you to neglect yourself and your needs to continue to be successful? Being successful is terrific; however, you need to balance the story. Make sure the story of success includes your family and friends, not just your career. Make sure it includes time for your personal renewal, creativity and relaxation.

As you continue on your journey as a leader, you must find methods and people to help you identify what your unchallenged internal stories and beliefs are. Discover them!

It may take some time to change your attitudes, thoughts, and feelings, as they have been engraved in your thinking by years of indoctrination, the repetition of *other people's* beliefs, and the internal stories you have been telling yourself. Some stories are lessons you learned—or misunderstood—and believed to be true for your entire life—so far. And now, here I am, trying to influence you into believing something totally alien to your original way of thinking. Why? To give you choices. To have more control of your filters and stories, you need to become aware of them. When you are aware of them, you can choose to accept, fine-tune or discard your internal stories. You become truer to yourself by learning more about your stories and choosing what *you* honestly think, believe and feel.

If you want to truly embrace your light and be a visible leader, explore these mindsets and filters because they are the internal stories you have built on what you already know, value, and believe—or think you do. We have all been influenced by the beliefs, feelings and emotions of other people. But just because someone else thinks a certain way does not mean *you* have to. Every invention ever made came because someone thought differently and was willing to try another way of doing things.

Because we filter the world through the internal map of our internal stories, and our point of view, we don't see what we are not aware of or looking for.

This means that as leaders, we must be open to other worldviews, cultures, and opinions to gain knowledge and a better interpretation of what is happening. This allows us to grow and stretch our internal stories into a more open, accepting, and inclusive view of the world. Our ability to find and apply knowledge in areas that are not a part of our current story could open our minds to many new possibilities. This willingness to be open and explore other ways of being will allow you to step into leadership. It may feel odd at first, especially if, like me, you have invisible roots from a culture where women are not allowed or encouraged to lead.

One researcher described internal stories that no longer work as people who, "have spent most of their lives committed to particular ways of thinking, doing, and being, and now [they] may find these approaches inadequate, unsatisfactory, or unworkable."[1] Recognizing when our internal stories are no longer working is not easy for us. But it is essential for our growth.

When our internal stories no longer work, we have two choices. We can build new or altered our internal stories if we are willing to embrace change. Or, we can decide that the very experience that shook our internal story was not applicable, ignore it and stay the same.

The process of becoming aware and questioning our internal stories can be an emotional, vulnerable time in life. When we are purposefully learning new skills, ways of thinking, and new ways of being, we can be in-between two stages of our development, and this can be a stressful and confusing state. This is when things we knew, or thought we are, become frayed or no longer relevant, because what we are learning does not align with our old way of thinking or being. It is a time of transition.

Remember, you get to choose what you believe, and who and how you will be. You will no longer blindly follow what you were taught, and what you heard from others. This is very much an act of being an adult—choosing who and what you are; and choosing your internal stories.

Conflict happens when we must choose between these two opposing internal stories, and it can be painful. Our minds strive to help us eliminate the pain as fast as possible. So, we may decide to ignore one option in favor of another. In such cases, we need to intimately explore our deeply held beliefs and consciously choose which beliefs (if any) to keep.

This will help us to confirm what our internal story will be, the story which supports our future self and helps to prepare us to lead. I had this internal story battle for about three years when I was thinking about becoming self-employed as the next step in my growth.

One story was I wanted to have more control of my schedule, time and work. My other story was, I loved the comfortable, easy, fun environment at the Harley-Davidson dealerships. So, I had a painful battle in my mind and heart for three years. I felt like a butterfly stuck in its chrysalis, trying to become something new, and felt uncomfortable with my desire for a new story that was different and unknown.

If we are not exposed to new, different ideas or challenges, we may not even be aware of the need to evaluate our internal stories. This will hold back our self-growth and delay us from reaching our potential as leaders and in life.

If, in my search for visible female leaders, I did not see female entrepreneurs leading their own businesses and controlling their lives, I would not have had another storyline option to consider. I also would not have had the long, three-year struggle of two conflicting stories. But I would not be where I am today, loving my new exciting entrepreneurial journey and the balance I have in my life.

What can you do to find new ideas, perspectives, or challenges to your internal stories? What have you seen other women doing and said to yourself, "I wish I could do that." That is the start of a new internal story, and if you are aware you can catch that wish and decide to make it a reality.

Take A Deep Breath and Reflect

As a leadership development facilitator, part of my role is to help you identify and question the internal stories you are telling yourself, and to provide guidance and support as you being to transition through your cognitive development.

Take a few minutes to think about the stories you have been telling yourself. Are there stories that at one time served you well, but now are holding you back?

It may be easier to start with the labels you have been assigned or allowed others to assign to you. Take a piece of paper and divide it down the middle. On one side, write Positive, and the other write Negative.

Now, set a timer, and for two to four minutes list all the words in the appropriate column that you use to describe yourself. If you had to describe yourself to someone who had never seen or met you before, what would you say?

Once the timer goes off, go over the words, and explore which words create the strongest feelings in your gut. Which word makes you excited? Which word makes you want to cry? Which words make you feel ashamed, or not good enough? Which words do you like to use when you describe yourself?

Now, examine the story behind how each of those words became assigned to you. As you identify each story, ask yourself, "Is that story still serving me? Is the story helping me to become the leader I am called to be? Is the story helping me to have the life I want to live? Or is this a story that is allowing me to keep my light from shining brightly for others to see?"

Take Action

Once you have identified and explored your stories, ask a trusted coach or mentor to listen to your stories and help you determine where the story may be holding you back from reaching your true potential as a leader. There are times when we need another person to help us identify the things we don't want to really acknowledge about ourselves. Having another, trusted person who listens and asks questions can help us reveal our deeper, invisible roots.

Finally, ask yourself, "Is it time to change some of my stories? What do I *want* my new stories to be?"

It is your life, and your chance to lead. What kind of person, and what kind of leader, do you choose to be?

Chapter 5
Your Whole Self

"If you're always trying to be normal, you will never know how amazing you can be." - Maya Angelou, American poet

Early in my career, I told my boss and mentor that I wanted to make a $100,000 per year someday. His advice was to find some female role models who were professionals I thought were making that much money and look at how they dressed, presented themselves, and behaved.

I did, and the process was extremely overwhelming. I was intimidated by the professional women's clothing, makeup, and accessories, not to mention the way they presented themselves. This overwhelm came from creating new potential internal stories that did not align with my old internal story about how I would present myself in the world. It stemmed back to being raised in the non-denominational Church of God and its rules for women. I grew up not being allowed to cut my hair, not wearing makeup, jewelry, or dresses above my knees, and had an absolute lack of caring about what I looked like.

Because I had been teased a lot about my appearance when I was in high school, I had somewhat of an attitude about the idea that people should like, appreciate, and respect me for my brains and what I can bring to the table. I thought the way I looked was not as important as who I was. I had to take a huge step back from the old internal story I had built in the church and high school to consider a new story about how I presented myself. It took me ten years, four image consultants, and a ton of internal self-love, encouragement, and work to change my old internal story.

I remember a conversation with my favorite image consultant, Rhoda Troyer, about dressing for my body type.

She said, "We match our image to how we see ourselves internally. If we don't love ourselves, if we are not confident, our body and how we are dressed is not going to be able to overcome the message we share unconsciously."

Rhoda taught me to dress for the body I have right now. She said, "Learn to feel good and be excited about the clothes that look good on you."

The other lessons I learned from Rhoda were about body language, presentation, and that the way I was holding myself were just as important as the way I was dressing, doing my makeup and my hairstyle.

Her focus on body language led me to dig deeper into our body language, and one of the biggest lessons I learned was not about what our bodies tell other people about us. It is about what our body language is telling us about our unconscious beliefs about ourselves.

When we think about the internal stories we tell ourselves, I believe it is essential to talk about another way we hold on to those stories. Often, in our western culture, we are taught to separate our minds and bodies, as if our body is not an essential and integral part of who we are. We are not made of a separate mind, spirit, and body. Each of us is a whole person; and all of us, our whole self, is needed to so we can grow and become all our Creator has called us to be. The reason I bring this up is because we need to feel, have emotions, and live in our bodies.

Richard Strozzi-Heckler tells us that, "Most of us live out lives that we've unconsciously inherited, and we're mimicking patterns of living that have been passed on to us by family, school, religion, government, economic institutions and the media." [1]

This unconscious inheriting of other people's beliefs and life patterns causes us to lose a valuable part of ourselves and we can go through our lives without even being aware of it. We are carrying other people's baggage within our whole self, in the stories we replay in our minds, and in our bodies, and it shows in the way we move and present ourselves to the world.

When I think about an example of this, I am reminded of a comment a dear friend of mine, Cathy G., made in the past year. She told me that when I first started working at the dealership, I walked with my head and eyes down and would not stop and talk to anyone. She saw that as I grew and developed as a leader I walked with my head up, greeting co-workers and smiling as I walked through the dealership. I changed how I carried myself. Cathy had observed and shared with me something I was not consciously aware of at the beginning of my leadership journey. She had seen my unconscious body language of being subservient and not worthy of being a leader.

I had to do a lot of work on how I present myself. In fact, there are times when I still struggle to look at people in their eyes, even when I am sharing something I am passionate about. When I catch myself, I give myself a gentle mind hug and remind myself, "I am a professional. I know what I am talking about. I have paid my dues. Aand I am good enough." Then I look the person in the eyes and continue speaking. If this is an area where you struggle too, remember to be kind to yourself while you unlearn years of embodying false beliefs about yourself and your ability to lead.

It is not just the disconnect from ourselves as a whole person that I think is important for us to understand. It is also the concept that we carry the stories we tell ourselves in our body and show them in the way we present ourselves to the world.

Richard Strozzi-Heckler shared multiple stories in his book which resonated within me, accounts of individuals who took their internal stories and labels—often unknowingly provided by other people—who allowed their whole selves to take on the shape of those constructs. So, each person had to relearn both their self-talk and their body language as they were changing their internal stories.

Amy Cuddy, in her famous TED Talk and in her book *Presence: Bringing Your Boldest Self to Your Biggest Challenges,* writes about how our bodies can change our minds. She encourages readers to practice power poses as a way to feel more empowered and confident. As we strive to become vibrant, visible female leaders, we need to be aware it is not just our minds, hearts, and souls that we need to work on it; is also our acceptance of our bodies. We have to embrace our whole selves, all of our perceived flaws, all of our perceived amazingness, and embody the leader we have been created to be.

In his book *Psycho-Cybernetics*, Maxwell Maltz shared that as he was doing plastic surgeries on people, he noticed that some of them, no matter how well the surgery went, would still believe the fixed part of their body was flawed. He shared the example of a woman who thought her nose was too big. Then, after he did the surgery to make it the perfect proportion, she still saw a big nose. This caused him to study psycho-cybernetics and uncover how our minds can override reality and affect how we view our bodies. Psycho-cybernetics means, "steering your mind to a productive, useful goal so you can reach the greatest port in the world, peace of mind." [2] We can become perfect, yet still see imperfections. This was a book one of my coaches had me read when I was working on improving my self-image, both mentally and physically.

Many of us struggle with loving our bodies just the way they are. We live in a culture that worships thin, perfect, and beautiful. Sometimes the media does promote good body images, but it is uncommon, and we have grown up with the burden, expectation, and untrue idea that our bodies need to be perfect. So, we may have a subliminal message programmed into us, and not be aware of its impact on our view of ourselves and how we present our whole selves to the world. If we don't address these beliefs, we will pass them on to the women who are following us on our leadership journey. Our daughters, nieces, and the girls who look up to us will assimilate our way of speaking about our bodies, our way of presenting ourselves, and pass it to the following generations.

Take A Deep Breath and Reflect

Take a mental inventory and think about your body. Do you love your whole self? Are you willing to wear a swimsuit on the beach? Are you ready to take pictures with your kids, your spouse, your family, and friends? Or do you pull back from those opportunities and miss opportunities to reveal a woman who loves herself and understands that she may become a different version of herself someday, but today this is who she is, and she will love her whole self and show that love to the world?

Take Action

Write a commitment in your reflective journal to work on the areas that you know you are struggling with regarding your body, your self-talk, and your image. Read that part of your journal, and remind yourself of this commitment each day.

Invisible Roots

Chapter 6
Self-Identity

"Whatever you do, you need to find your tribe. If you are a zebra, find the zebras and run with them. If you are a gazelle, then find the herd that runs at your pace. If you are a lion, find your pride. Finding your tribe is not about being of the same color or same ethnicity or same history; it's about being one of heart and mind."
– Erwin Raphael McManus, The Last Arrow

I believe developing as leader, at its core, is an in-depth transformational process. It requires us to embody leadership, to believe and identify ourselves as being leaders.

This type of development may require a profound change in your worldviews, beliefs, stories, labels, and ways of being in the world. It requires us to build our leadership identities. We can be tempted focus on "knowing *that*," or objective knowledge gained from books, seminars, and podcasts; but we cannot master the "know *how*" knowledge or embody being a leader through those methods. Paul Duguid states it this way: "Learning about only requires the accumulation of knowledge...which confers the ability to talk a good game, but not necessarily to play one." [1]

While practice and knowledge help us to become more confident as leaders until we believe in and identify ourselves as being leaders, we will still be hiding our light. If we are going to become visible leaders, we need to have a deeper understanding of ourselves. We need to gain knowledge, take action, and embody leadership. We need to feel in our whole selves that we are leaders, and be able to stand and say out loud, and through our actions, "I am a leader."

As we develop a mindset that can deal with more complexity, our identity begins to evolve and develop. Through this process, our leadership identity becomes assimilated and ingrained. I'd like you to notice the word assimilated. One of the definitions of assimilating is, "to absorb into the cultural tradition of a population or group." Assimilation is not about choosing; it is about being absorbed. This means if you feel the call to lead, and you grew up in an unsupportive environment, it is going to take work for you to verbally and mentally identify yourself as a leader. If I ask you right now, "Are you a leader?" what would your answer be?

Did you just mentally list all the reasons you are not a leader? It is ok if you did, but that means you need to reprogram your beliefs and your identity.

And now I have some excellent news: self-identity does not stop evolving when we become adults. Research by Erikson shows that our self-identity continues to develop throughout adulthood. We can continue to change our identity through internal work.

The development of self-identity can happen at different times, depending on our environment and interests. Developing self-identity is a complex process in which we develop an understanding of ourselves as individuals and of ourselves within our social and cultural environment.

The answers to the question, "Who am I?" can include personal and professional goals, behavioral patterns, preferences, and characteristics we relate to ourselves. Some of us can develop an identity associated with where we work or the type of work we do. Others develop an identity such as "I'm Marcus's mom," or "I'm Dan's wife." While these identities are true and accurate, they should not become our core identity. If we allow these identities to become our core, we lose our understanding of who we are as women and as individuals.

We need to do the work to have our own identity, a self-identity that is stronger than being a part of our workgroup or our family.

Creating this type of self-identity can require more profound personal work on our part. I have spoken to many women who communicated that their core identity used to circle around their work and their family. Then, when their company downsized, or their kids moved away, they became lost and no longer sure of who they are as individuals. If you have a stronger core identity that is just about you as a strong, vibrant woman who leads, these challenges to who you are as a person are not as dramatically shocking. It is easier to adapt when you know who you are in your core. Your core identity needs to be about you, not you in relation to someone or something else. For example, "I am a smart, hardworking, caring woman who enjoys helping others by taking a leadership role," or "I am a good-hearted, compassionate woman who needs to find out who I am and achieve my potential."

Social influences on self-identity

Your tribe and the environment in which you are developing your leadership can both influence your self-identity as a leader. These social environments, the people we spend time with, and the organizations we are involved with all create a shared identity. They also create a shared system of classification including information about social positions and statuses, such as age, class, gender, religion, or race. The social situations in which we choose to function have direct consequences for our sense of self and affect our self-identity as a leader. If we are in a social environment that does not support us becoming a strong female leader, it is much harder to embody the identity of a visible female leader. Find an environment that is open and encouraging to women in leadership. Ask the question when you are being interviewed. Understand what they are doing to help individuals develop their leadership identity and skills.

Some companies are actively seeking to help women step into their industries. Abigail Johnson from Fidelity shared in an interview that they believe diversity in business is imperative. Diversity is the way to position organizations to thrive. She explained that her company views women as a critical part of the future of financial services.[2] Other companies are also working to create supportive environments for women. IBM has a formal mentoring program for women. ADP hosts an Executive Women in Leadership conference.

If the situation you are in is not right for you, do something about it. Take a chance. You may have to change your internal story to be open to new opportunities.

I remember that there was a constant battle between my identity as a young female who felt called to lead and the environment around me; it taught me that women were expected to be subservient to men. As I think back to what it was like being in that environment, I believe if I had stayed, I could have become bitter and would now feel very unfulfilled. I could have taken on a victim identity and certainly would not have achieved my potential as a leader.

Fortunately, I chose to spend my time—by making a conscious choice—in different environments that have supported my sense of who I am meant to be and what I have been called to do.

Relationships built within an organization or social environments can also influence our awareness and confidence in practicing leadership. The relationships we have can help us to develop. These relationships allow us to begin to understand ourselves as a mosaic of the many different aspects of who we are through interactions with different people.

As you choose to connect with yourself as a leader, you must find your tribe. Our tribes are different for each of us. Our tribe is a group of people who love and support us, who ask us the hard questions, and who (figuratively) give us a good swift kick in the behind when we need it. They support us and help us to grow, as women and as leaders.

For a long time, I felt discouraged about finding my tribe. I had a hard time finding a group that fit my ideas and goals. I discovered that one tribe, one single group, is not the perfect fit for me. Instead, I became an honorary member of many tribes. These tribes included groups that encouraged and engaged my creativity, tribes that supported and engaged my nerdy self, and tribes that embraced my unique way of being in the world and helped me to be fully myself with all my different interests. This is what you need to find.

Seek the people who build you up, who push you further and cheer for you. As my friend Cassie says, "Find people who want to compliment, not complete." Then, once you find your tribe, or tribes, find other female leaders and invite them into your tribe. Your invitation can influence their leadership self-identity by acknowledging their potential, encouraging their awareness and acceptance of leadership, provide useful feedback, and help them to build a sense of themselves as leaders and as women.

There is a point in everyone's development where they will need other people's influence to stimulate their growth. The other people offer alternate stories to the ones you are living. When other people provide feedback that confirming your leadership efforts are acceptable, and when they acknowledge your leadership skills, it reinforces their leader self-identity—and yours. Marillyn Hewson shared that her mother was the one who influenced her in business and leadership and taught her the value of money. [3]

Social feedback validates your acceptance of yourself as a leader. It reinforces the new stories you are trying to bring into your life. Marillyn's mom helped to reinforce her daughter's identity as a business leader who understands the value of money.

Feedback helps us to firm up our self-identities. If others do not accept our attempts to change it may be much more difficult for us to emerge and establish ourselves as leaders, emotionally, physically and mentally. Your ability to gain awareness of yourself as a leader, build self-confidence in your leadership skills by using them successfully, and receive positive feedback from other people will impact and help you to develop your leadership self-identity. In an interview with CNBC, Ginni Rometty, the Chairman, President, and CEO of IBM, said that her mom taught her not to let someone else define who she is. She stated that IBM works to keep women in the workforce and to support their leadership growth. [4]

So, choose your tribes wisely because they have influence; but ultimately, we need to develop our own internal leadership practice and define ourselves as leaders.

Developing a leadership identity within a social environment is essential since leadership involves a leader, their followers, and the environment. Leadership is "a process of social influence, to guide, structure and/or facilitate behaviors, activities, and/or relationships towards the achievement of shared aims."[5]

There is also a point where we need to separate ourselves from the social environment around us and stand on our own. Each of us needs the support of others to build our identity as a leader, and then we need to learn to give up our dependence on others and bolster our self-identity.

Becoming independent from the social influences that supported the development of our identity as a leader can be challenging, painful, and time-consuming. This choosing of independence is a necessary growth path which moves us from a socialized mindset to one based on the self-authored or self-transformational mind. We develop a mindset that allows us to find and create new and inspirational internal stories— stories that allow us to live the amazing lives we desire.

The ability to separate ourselves from external influences and make our own choices is essential. It will allow you to make decisions as a leader that are not popular but are the right decision. Without independence in your thinking you will always seek the approval of others, whether you are aware of the seeking or not.

As we develop our separate identities, we also need to develop the ability to recognize and question our internal authorities, the old stories playing through our hearts, minds, and bodies. The ability to create space and separate from our internal authorities, or the stories we tell ourselves, allows us to understand that we only see a part of the stories, and that there are other pieces we need to collect in order to see more or differently. This is vital in our leadership development.[6]

Learning to be independent from both external and internal influences gives us the ability to cultivate a broader view of the world in which we are learning to lead, and it facilitates moving to the next level of our cognitive development.

Take A Deep Breath and Reflect

If you have made a wish for more women leaders, you are being called to be a leader yourself.

Who are you spending time with? Do they support you and encourage you to become a visible leader, or do they allow or encourage you to hide your gifts?

Sometimes we need someone who is not close to us to see our gifts and point them out to us.

Now, think about the social environments in which you interact with others. Are you putting yourself into situations where you will meet other leaders? Do you bring all your leadership gifts, or do you mask them so others will not feel uncomfortable? Do you have someone who encourages you to bring your leadership gifts? If I asked you, "are you a leader?" would you own this identity or give me all the reasons why you are not a leader?

How you identify yourself matters. You will find it can be hard to identify other emerging leaders' gifts if you cannot connect with your own leadership gifts. Do you need to work with a leadership coach or a mentor to help you dive deeper into your personal leadership development?

Take Action

In your reflection journal write a list of all the identities you currently have. Make a list of the characteristics you would like to add to your list. Double-check your list, and make sure the identities on both lists are ones that you want to keep. If there are any that do not belong on your lists, make a plan to recognize and stop your association with that internal story whenever and wherever it pops up in your life.

Find another aspiring leader and help reinforce their leadership self-identity. You can point out specific leadership traits you have seen them use to help them and encourage their self-identity as a leader.

Chapter 7
Renewing Our Spirit

"If you can't figure out your purpose, figure out your passion. For your passion will lead you right into your purpose." — T.D. Jakes

It may seem odd to include renewing our spiritual self as part of your path to growing and developing as a visible female leader. However, spiritual growth is essential. It opens opportunities for us to discover our higher purpose, renew our core self, and find our *why*. Simon Sinek often talks about the importance of finding your why, which is the reason companies and leaders do what they do. Our why is a deeper, more meaningful, thoughtful reason for aspiring to be a leader. French philosopher Teilhard de Chardin (1881-1955) said, "We are not human beings having a spiritual experience. We are spiritual beings having a human experience."[1]

Because the words spiritual and religion are often used interchangeably, it is essential to understand that spirituality and religion are distinct, if overlapping, constructs. Often, religion focuses on rules and ideology, whereas spirituality focuses on relationships with a higher power. Having a personal connection or experience with the divine builds our awareness of the existence and experiences of our inner feelings and beliefs, which helps to shape the meaning, purpose, and mission in our daily lives. Spirituality is about understanding and developing a sense of interconnectedness between all things, a sense of healing and wholeness. Also, religions are communities of faith organized to provide openings to their sacred and meaningful community rituals, whereas spirituality focuses on the journey toward wholeness that you must take to realize your potential. These differing opportunities for experiences allow us to grow and develop into our whole, authentic self.

As we become influential leaders we need to find the experiences, people, activities, and practices which feed our spiritual being. Without these, the nurturing part of us withers and dies, and we are not whole. Developing a more in-depth spiritual self requires different conditions for different people. The things that help one woman develop and cultivate her whole self may hinder another. Spirituality is a part of our identity, and it helps us build authenticity. The ability to explore authenticity, meaning, purpose and mission in daily life allows us to develop our leadership and gain a more profound understanding of ourselves, the environments surrounding us, and those environments we choose to be in.

The next chapter will take a deeper dive into what the authentic self is. Our spiritual renewal supports leadership mastery. When we are living to our full potential, we can lead from a place of abundance. When we experience a connection with the larger universe and with others, we begin to understand that we are a part of a whole, not the whole itself. Spirituality is an integral part of the entire developmental process.

This type of growth connects us with how we make meaning, and that we can create a sense of being whole and connected in all things.[2] The wholeness that is created by spiritual renewal facilitates us creating our self-identity and the construction of knowledge. As spiritual beings, we participate in an endless search for growth; thus, "spirituality evolves and changes, as do our needs, in light of our experiences, our changing understanding of our experiences, and our changing relationships to self, others, and the larger environment."[3] Spirituality can be seen as a vital element of being human, and just as the human body and mind develop and grow, so does a human spirit.

Spiritual development can become a part of transformational learning. When we learn and find openness within our core selves, with other perspectives, other people, and all the other possibilities, it fuels our transformation.[2] Developing spiritually is about you strengthening your core self, the core that connects with a higher power, the abundant universe, and people. Becoming a spiritual being is a learning process which happens as a part of everyday life.

Spirituality renewal can be nurtured through the use of artistic activities and creativity, such as art, poetry, music, literature, storytelling, and visualization. I found a connection to my spirituality in a love to paint, draw, quilt, melt glass, and have new creative experiences. It can also be found in merely enjoying your favorite coffee in a café you love, or through activities exploring nature and cultures that are different from yours. You may find your connection to spirituality comes from religious practices such as prayer or meditation.

Spirituality is what fills your soul, makes you feel alive, gives you energy, and makes your soul sing. During my spiritual journey I needed to learn to find joy in my life, to find beauty in the dandelions dotting the front yard, the weeds, and the other things I can't control. I found it in learning to sincerely celebrate other people's successes, in the art that I create, and the art I admire. I have found it when walking in the woods by myself and with others. I had to learn to *be* at peace, not just to search for it.

I believe each of us finds our connection to the Creator and to our higher purpose in our own unique ways. I have been using the phrase "embrace your journey" for years, as the salutation on my emails, letters, and books. That is what spiritual development and our higher purpose means to me.

Your spiritual growth is about embracing the journey —each piece, including the parts we love and the parts we hate, the pauses, the winding, the challenges, and the joys— and embracing them all equally.

Take A Deep Breath and Reflect

How are you embracing your spiritual development? What nurtures you?

What have you stopped doing that you used to love, that thing that made you feel alive, connected, and a part of something bigger than you?

When was the last time you did a technology detox? Leave all technology off for three days and just be, and celebrate the joy of being.

Often, when I have this conversation with women, they tell me stories of giving up art, music, nature walks, or time with their Creator to serve their families and fulfill what they have seen as their roles and responsibilities.

I use this adage often: you have to put your own mask on first. When you lose your connection to a higher purpose, or when you lose your creative, personal time, you lose a crucial part of what makes you amazing. You lose a part of what and who you are.

One lady shared with me that she had stopped riding her motorcycle, something she loved to do, after her kids were born, because she was trying to be a "normal" mom. When we stop doing what we love to conform, we are not our true selves, and we lose an essential piece of who we really are.

So, what do you need to make time for in your life, to reconnect to your higher purpose? What do you need to do to renew yourself?

Take Action

Set a date and commit to a technology detox. If that makes you nervous, start small. Leave your phone in the car when you go out to dinner, and practice really connecting and being present with the people you are with. When you are ready for a more significant challenge, try a technology-free day or weekend.

Set a date, and commit to doing something you love just for the joy of it. Then, in your reflection journal, write about your experience.

Chapter 8
The Journey Towards Leadership

"To thrive and to innovate in today's complex, globally connected world, leaders need sophisticated ways to step back to understand what they are facing within and outside themselves." - Daniel Vasella, Chairman, Novartis

As you are taking your leadership development journey, it is vital to understand the importance of what you are doing—developing yourself as a leader, on purpose. The fact you are reading this book is an indication that you have a calling be a directional marker on someone else's map, to take charge and lead yourself in embracing the higher purpose you were created for.

Our leadership growth can happen anywhere and at any time. We can have experiences in our day-to-day lives, whether at home or at work, that are the same as what we experience within a program, but we can view the experiences and what we learn differently. Within a program or a purposeful leader and leadership development, the stage is set for viewing the situations, interactions, and information presented through a learner's mindset.

A leadership development facilitator can help you to create a learner's mindset lens through which everyday occurrences are viewed as opportunities to grow and learn as a leader. This lens is designed to assist learners to become aware of their habitual ways of interacting with their everyday stories and experiences.

Preparing for learning, being open to everyday learning experiences, and building an awareness of how internal stories influence how we view our experiences are all critical in leadership development. While preparation is essential, my research has raised my perception of the responsibility of being a leadership development practitioner and of the work it can take to develop as a leader.

As both a practitioner and a woman who is walking this path, I understand that the journey to grow as a leader is not comfortable. It includes emotions and feelings, not just information and observational learning. There can be an emotional cost as you decide to pursue becoming a leader who practices living and embracing a full life. Leader and leadership development can challenge you emotionally, cognitively, spiritually, physically, and can shake your private foundations. You must have a robust internal leadership practice that helps you while you are experiencing growth.

We will talk about this practice again in Chapter 10.

As you build your leadership practice, and you answer the call to become the leader you are meant to be, there will be struggles and challenges. Many of them will be internal struggles because you may find yourself challenging beliefs you have absorbed or held your entire life. I assure you, these feelings and the struggle are normal.

When you engage in this type of transformation, you are experiencing transformational learning. The process of transformational learning may happen like this: first, we may experience a disorienting dilemma which causes us to question our long-held beliefs and assumptions. This starts the cycle for our personal transformation.

We may see a woman who is standing in her light as a leader, living a full and abundant life. And we think, "I should do that." Or "I wish I…" Then we think, "I can't do that." Later, as we continue to admire the way she is living her life, we ask "Why can't I do that?"

Next, we may look around and find others who are more experienced in living full and abundant lives and who have had similar experiences, and we talk to them. We begin to "try on" what it would look like if we led in our own way, celebrating our leadership gifts. As we try on this new identity we begin to create a course of action which will allow us to gather the skills, knowledge, and courage it will take to become the type of leader we believe the world needs. We then take this knowledge and start using it in small ways and practice the skills. As we get feedback from our tribe, we begin to find more courage and self-confidence in our abilities. Then we integrate this new way of being or believing in our life based on our unique perspective. We become that leader.

I bring up transformational learning because as I was striving to become a visible leader, I had to go through this transformational learning process. In my case, I can attest to it being a long, painful process. I think any time we are challenging our long-held beliefs it is a hard and emotional process. Even when we don't agree with the long-held beliefs, uprooting them can take hard work.

These beliefs, even when we have mentally rejected them, have invisible roots that curl into the deep parts of our heart, soul, and body. They keep sending us unconscious messages of being unworthy, not good enough, or having nothing to offer, and suggesting that we are not leaders.

In my mind, I did not agree with the idea that women could not be leaders. However, I had years of that belief written on my heart, my soul, and I embodied that belief. So, it should not be surprising that it took me a long time and a lot of work to undo those beliefs. I had to use verbal, written, and mental mantras to help me hear the truth I knew but could not yet embody. I went through several disorienting dilemmas related to myself as a leader and how I was hiding my gifts so I would not make others feel intimated by my presence. I was hiding my gifts so I would not conflict with the old internal stories related to how women were expected to be.

I had some beliefs so profoundly hidden and deeply rooted that I could not do all the work of rejecting them by myself because I could not see them—but I could feel the way they held me back from being the leader I wanted to become. So, I worked with several talented coaches. One coach in particular, Cathy Geib, really challenged me to peel my onion. (My phrase, not hers.) The phrase resonates with what I felt I went through as I was going through this phase of transformational learning. It felt like there were lots of layers, and lots of tears, which is how I think about peeling onions. That journey took me a long time, but it was worth the time and effort I went through to be where I am today.

We need that level of commitment to peeling our personal onions because transformational learning is a process of changing our attitudes, opinions, and the beliefs making up our deeply held internal stories. This level of transformation and growth requires a higher purpose, a big why.

Cathy was able to hear the message under the words I was saying, and she was able to catch the underlying root message I was still giving myself because of the culture I had grown up in. She was able to challenge beliefs I did not even know I was still holding, and she helped me start the process of digging out the deeper, invisible roots and cutting them cleanly.

The transformational journey and our understanding

of what we experience is different for each of us. It could be experienced emotionally and intuitively by one person while others encounter it logically and rationally. No matter how we experience transformational learning, a profound shift in our perspective happens, and it helps us to choose internal stories focusing on the women we want to be, on our future selves, living the lives we choose.

During the learning process, social interactions are vital since interaction helps us observe and understand other ways of viewing the world and situations. I needed a coach, and mentors. Friends who believed in me did not let me off the hook, and they both challenged and supported me.

Transformational learning is one of the deep processes of developing ourselves, and having outside support is crucial. This process is not a fast, easy fix for becoming a visible leader. But if you are not currently leading in the way you feel you are being called to lead, it's likely that you will have to do this more in-depth work to uncover the invisible roots holding you back. Transformational learning offers the potential for lasting transformational change within the women who participate in the process. Having a supportive coach, or a supportive community, is essential.

Interacting with people who are different, who think differently from what we are accustomed to, and who have had different experiences than ours allows us to become more aware of different ways of thinking and being within the world. This can happen within a social context, and it can include many levels of interactions, skills, knowledge, and values. And within this activity, we may experience conflicts between our past and current internal stories, our culture, family, peer groups, and personal experiences influence our values and preferences. These influences help to cement our internal stories, whether they are positive or negative.

Just because we are embracing experiences of different ways of being in the world does not mean we are prepared or able to make the shift. *The Short and Tragic Life of Robert Peace* by Jeff Hobbs is just one example of many.[1] I have heard this story told many different ways by different people, stories of young men and women from lower-income communities who receive scholarships and leave to find better opportunities. Then return to the same situation after graduating because they did the scholarly work to move to the next level but not the internal work on the stories they tell themselves.

The problem was that they kept the same internal stories, and they were not even aware these stories needed to be updated as well. These individuals, and there were many of them, needed to experience their own transformational learning, and learn to view themselves and their worlds through different lenses. They had gained book learning and scholarly knowledge; but for some reason, they were not able to process the more profound life lessons. They were not able to transform into a version of themselves as successful people within the new opportunities they were offered.

This same thing can happen to us as we are in the process of creating our leadership self-identity. We can learn all of the words, mannerisms, and interpersonal leadership skills, but if we fail to do the deep work, the intrapersonal work, we can end up right back where we started.

As we gain self-awareness, relationships can help us in the transformational learning process. It has been said that growth is "not an independent act but is an interdependent relationship built on trust."[2] Transformational learning helps us to understand, on a deep level, how social influences have impacted the way we view the world, other people, and even ourselves, causing us to challenge our current internal stories. This awareness may trigger the transformational learning process. But without disorienting dilemmas or other triggering events, we rarely experience transformational learning. And although it helped me to move to my next level, it was not a comfortable or pleasant experience.

Even when you are open to growing in this new way, you may not experience challenges to your current internal stories within your existing social and cultural environment to trigger the transformational process. Some people have lived their entire lives within a couple of miles of where they were born and raised. They mirror the relationship their parents had once they were married. They raise their kids the same way they were raised, with the same rules and consequences. They have never or rarely meet people who are from different cultures, or who are significantly different from their neighbors or themselves. They work at the same job, have the same routine, go to the same ball games, eat the same food, and never experience challenges to their status quo. Living this type of life in the same environment, they rarely experience challenges or pressures that prompt them to acknowledge or examine their assumptions about themselves, their community or their society.[3]

Without choosing to discover other cultures, other ways of thinking and being in the world, you will not become any different. When you make the decision that something needs to change you may have to look outside your current environment, social circle and way of being in the world. Without a purposeful intent you can be stuck in a rut and not even realize that you are not growing and becoming a better version of yourself.

If you don't believe this statement, use your cell phone and turn on a Google Maps timeline and allow it to track your movements for a couple of months. Then, look at where you spend your time. I have had mine on for years; I have spent most of my time in Ohio, and some time on the east coast, but very little time west of the Mississippi.

It is hard to be exposed to different ways of thinking if we are surrounded by people who think the same as we do. If we are not exposed to a different way of thinking or being, how can we move to our next level as leaders? Our awareness increases and presents opportunities to develop our whole self within the challenges we experience. This exposure to a disorienting dilemma does not happen in isolation, but instead originates from our interactions within a social community. Transformational learning requires something or someone to offer challenges to our current internal stories, someone who can hear and challenge the stories we are telling ourselves. Transformational learning can help us to develop a new identity that we consciously choose, and create our awareness of self, thus enhancing our individuality by separating us from the group and using our new awareness to build an authentic connection and a genuine union with who we truly are.

Even when we experience challenges to our current internal stories and become aware of a need to shift our existing internal stories to more inclusive and leadership-centered filter, the shift may not be a natural process. Transformational learning is not a rational process, and it can be a highly sensitive, personal process. For that reason, transformational learning requires us to be open to questioning the perspectives we develop from our experiences and to begin a process to change or offer a different view of our current encounters. Through awareness, reflection, making sense of changes, and taking action based on a new internal story, we engage in transformative learning.

As a woman who is striving to become an influential leader, you can easily go from one extreme to another. If you have felt for years that you have been suppressed, that your leadership gifts have been undervalued, you may believe that being louder is the way to be heard.

Here is the reality: your leadership is the way you live. It is how you connect and touch other people's lives so you can influence their future, and even their future generations. Leadership is how you choose to live your life; it is embracing your impossible dreams and pulling them into possibility. It is embracing who you are, who your future self will be and loving them both.

With your life example, you will touch some people's lives for a moment, and then you will never see or talk to them again. But by being a visible leader who celebrates and embraces your leadership gifts, you are modeling what a successful woman in leadership looks like. At that moment, you are planting the thought in other people's minds that they can be a leader as well. You are showing that they can choose new internal stories for the lives they want to live.

You may find that as you practice your personal leadership you will connect with others and be a part of their lives going forward. You are planting a directional marker on their map. You are providing inspiration and opportunities for them to become aware, to begin their own leadership journey because of their interactions with you.

We can touch people's lives just by being present, by modeling an internal leadership practice, by remembering and honoring the whole person. As we model leadership for others, demonstrating that we are more than one dimensional, we are embracing our own leadership journey, and we are showing them the path for them to do the same. If we reflect on it, this message contains internal stories from our head, heart, body, and spirit. When we actively choose our internal stories we show others that they can do it too.

It takes some courage to choose a leadership path, to decide to have a leadership practice, and to begin a path of growth and change—and to decide to take this path and be visible and vulnerable while you are on your journey. It is ok to feel vulnerable, and you do not need to have all the answers as you begin; you will find them during your journey.

As you touch people's lives, you remind them that they are not alone and they will have support as they walk the path. But ultimately the journey is up to them. They are the only ones who can take their path and find the courage to embrace change even when it is hard for them, just as you are the only one who can take your journey. You can model what it is like to love yourself, even the aspects you don't like or view as weaknesses. You can model how to embrace change even when it is hard, emotionally challenging, and you don't really want to face the challenges.

Don't feel that this is all up to you. As I was called to write this book, I was also convinced that the ability to learn and practice leadership applies to me as well. I needed to live my full life, choosing my internal stories that support the woman I want to be in the future. Even current leaders who feel called to help others on their leadership growth journey must use the same practices to lead and model living a full life without an assigned script. We too must be willing to love and accept ourselves, even the parts we view as weaknesses. We must be willing to accept that there is no clear path laid out for our personal leadership journey and still be prepared to travel it regardless of whether we feel scared, excited, discouraged, or ready. This is the foundation for leadership development, and leadership practice. It is the foundation for living a life we love.

Take A Deep Breath and Reflect

As you think about being called to become a visible leader, what feelings, emotions, and thoughts does that bring up in you? Have you been seeking out ways to develop yourself that will help you to become the leader you are meant to be? Or have you been avoiding doing anything, and hoping that the feeling will go away?

This may be the season in your life when you start to prepare yourself and get ready to lead. What are you doing to prepare? What are you doing to share what you are learning with those who are coming behind you on their leadership journeys?

Take Action

After you have assessed what season you are in, open your reflection journal and list five ways you are going to celebrate and enjoy this season to its fullest. Think of the dreams and the vision you have for your future. Then list three ways you are going to prepare for the next season of your life.

Chapter 9
Opening Our Awareness

"The first step toward change is awareness. The second step is acceptance."
- Nathaniel Branden

A s you decide to take the challenge and step into being the leader you are called to be, there is work you need to do about becoming aware. There are two areas of awareness I believe you must master: building awareness of others, and developing an awareness of yourself. Developing this awareness muscle helps you to take notice and not ignore the subtle messages conveyed both by you and by others.

Awareness of Others

Being able to observe and see what is happening inside the situations in which you are called to lead, and in the people who make up the organizations, is essential to building your awareness of others. It is this awareness which allows you to gain insights into what is happening, why it may be happening, and how you are influencing the situation. Some researchers refer to this as being able to sense what is happening within a situation or environment and it is the ability to be aware within a situation. It is the ability to detect and be mindful of the situation and the people who are involved.

The more you are aware of others, and the more you can identify the differences between what they say and what they truly think and feel, and the more you can influence their growth. What are they not saying? Do they agree to something just to go along with everyone else, or do they really agree? What has not been said that should be known or discussed?

Self-Awareness

Your awareness of yourself is an essential part of an internal leadership practice. You may have been exposed to the concept of leadership before, but perhaps leadership was filtered out of your consciousness because it did not fit the stories you have been telling yourself, or the restrictions placed on you by others. Your understanding of your own identity, spiritual development, and mindset can all influence other people's abilities to access and enhance their self-awareness. As you become aware of the need to be influential and visible in your leadership, this awareness will challenge you to start the process of building your own internal leadership practice. To gain this awareness we must interact with the cultures we find ourselves in, or choose to be part of, and other people. This will help us to begin the process of becoming aware of ourselves and the areas of knowledge, understanding, practice or compassion in which we need to grow and develop.

Self-awareness is often encouraged as individuals are striving to grow and develop. However, self-awareness can be imperfect because of our perceptions of ourselves. Our perceptions are usually relative to the standards of others. For example, a woman drawn to leadership may think she is not subservient enough according to the dictates of her church, but as a leader being subservient can cause issues. We need to check our perceptions against something or someone else. Chapter 10 offers suggestions for how to check these perceptions.

As we grow and develop our leadership practice we can use our life filters, leadership gifts and leadership identity to help as a measuring tool for the type of person and leader we want to be. Bill George, in *Discover Your True North,* tells us that becoming self-aware is half of the challenge. Even when we become self-aware, we still need to learn to accept ourselves. He states, "with self-awareness, accepting your authentic self becomes much easier. You see yourself clearly and accurately, and you know what you truly believe."[1] Accepting who we truly are, with our perceived and actual flaws, imperfectness, and challenges are what can take us to our next level.

When I think about my experiences with self-awareness and learning to accept myself, I think back to when I was first trying to become a leader. I was just trying to be successful and, in some ways, I was not kind to myself as I was trying to become a better leader. I was hard on myself because of what I perceived as my flaws and areas where I needed to grow. As I reflect on my younger self, I look at her with love and admiration. If she had not been willing to go through those hard, internal changes, I would not be where I am today.

Experience as a leader and maturity have led to me becoming more gracious and patient with myself and my leadership growth path. I believe our small efforts to increase our self-awareness can help us to assess and self-regulate in more meaningful and impactful ways. These allow us to see areas where we can learn, grow and become more effective leaders while also being positive about ourselves in the process.

As we are becoming more self-aware, we begin to self-regulate; that is, we judge or evaluate our performance based on benchmarks or the performance of others. This is why we must surround ourselves with examples of effective leadership. When we are around a group of successful leadership role models, we can assess our performance against theirs, using their examples as benchmarks, and strive for the same level of success that our role models have achieved. If you are around leaders who are struggling you might end up observing and modeling the behaviors that duplicate their struggle.

Jim Rohn said, "we are the average of the five people we spend the most time with."[2] Research also shows that we are influenced by the people we interact with, and we become more like them. There are times when we need others and their influence on us to help us develop, and enhance, our self-awareness and mastery of skills. Even when we are self-aware we may not realize that there are specific areas where we need to develop and to stretch ourselves. We need others who can help us to identify that we are missing certain skills or abilities. It is through interaction with other leaders that we become aware of our blind spots and choose to work on them.

Blind Spots
Blind spots are "[the] things we don't want to know about ourselves."[3] Sometimes they are things we can't know about ourselves because our internal stories and filters don't allow us to see them. These blind spots can block the learning we need to break through our old filters and create an awareness that the current internal story no longer works for us. Achieving this breakthrough can be challenging if we rely solely on ourselves for awareness and growth. When we rely only on our self-awareness, and unstructured, self-

directed learning we may encounter blind spots in our knowledge related to our internal stories, worldviews, assumptions, needs, and responsibilities concerning our blind spots.

Since we all have blind spots, we need to develop strategies to identify and counterbalance blind spots founded on flawed, old internal stories. We need intervention from other leaders, and we need to make a balanced, thoughtful reflection so we can identify the assumptions we make and whether they are correct or incorrect.

Thoughtful reflection is not about looking for the negative or focusing on what is wrong. Instead, it is about taking an in-depth, objective look at situations and events. This process is essential to transformational learning since our internal stories can be constructed experiences that we have involuntarily assimilated from the people and culture around us.[4] Since our internal stories affect how we see, understand and interpret situations, expanding our awareness by being open to different points of view allows us to develop an internal story that is open to success, inclusion and self-love.

I remember one blind spot a mentor made me aware of. It was in the way I speak, and I did not realize it was incorrect. I grew up in a small community where this grammar mistake is widespread, so it sounded correct to me. When I saw something, I would say, "I seen the dog," instead of "I have seen the dog." Since my mentor knew I wanted to do presentations and teach, he pointed it out to me. This may come as a shock to those of you who know me, but I did not believe him, so I googled it and discovered he was correct. Once I knew about this, I had to find a way to change my phrasing. However, I could not catch myself saying it; I was so used to speaking that way I didn't notice it when I made a mistake. So, I asked my mentor to help, and he was gracious enough to correct me when he heard me saying it until I could catch it myself. This process took about eight months. If he hadn't pointed it out to me, I would have never known I was not speaking correctly because of a blind spot.

Take A Deep Breath and Reflect

Part of this awareness comes as a result of thoughtful reflection, which will be discussed in more detail in Chapter 10. However, there is another piece of this, and that is the ability to listen to what is being said and what is *not* being said, what is shared, and what is held back. This comes with the practice of being aware within situations. While this seems straightforward, it takes a lot of practice because it is easy to get involved in the conversation and miss the opportunity to reflect-in-action.

Who do you have in your life that points out your blind

spots in a kind way? Who do you have who challenges you to be more aware of yourself and others? What do you think you need to do to improve your awareness?

Take Action

The purpose of this exercise is to help you develop and strengthen your awareness muscles.

In the next meeting, or group environment that you are in, or other appropriate situation, take three pieces of paper. Label the first piece Me. You will use this page to make notes about how you are feeling and what you observe about yourself. Label the second page Others. This page is where you write down what you observe in other people, both their verbal and nonverbal behavior. Then label the third page Room. On this page you will make notes about the environment.

After the meeting, review your notes. Notice what you were aware of, then ask yourself, "what did I miss?" If you identify anything you think you missed, try to be more aware of it in the next meeting.

Chapter 10
Your Internal Leadership Practice

". . . to be a more effective leader, you must be yourself—more—with skill."
- Goffee and Jones

Ultimately, we want to become leaders who can lead without needing to follow a predetermined script, to become women who model full, vibrant lives, and that takes internal personal work. When we are self-aware and actively seek growth opportunities, we bring our gifts and strengths and multiply them by influencing others to do the same. I often view this type of growth as an internal leadership practice.

An internal leadership practice requires discipline, awareness, openness, honesty, and curiosity. It takes some courage to be willing to be uncomfortable and challenged. One of my students, Thomas Montgomery, once told me "growth comes through stepping into the uncomfortable places." This practice of stepping into uncomfortable places is about more than the moves and actions a leader takes. It is about becoming a person who embodies leadership in all areas of our lives, in our whole self. It is about choosing the type of life we want to live and doing the work to change our old internal stories, and stop them from holding us back from achieving our true potential.

An internal leadership practice embodies the whole of what leadership is through self-identity, cognitive and spiritual awareness, and through knowledge, action, and ultimately becoming a leader.

Like a yoga practice, this type of development does not require you to be a master the first day. Practice and instruction are needed. The practice is internal, it happens within us; and the instruction is external, coming from a practitioner who guides the practice. This is a person who has walked the path before us—they have already become a leader—and is showing us the way.

We will not know all the answers, the techniques, the flow of the movements, but we must be willing to learn. We carry all we discover within us. We build on the practice by learning the basics and moving towards mastery. With each year, each experience, each self-reflection there is more growth, more nuances understood and mastered, and more opportunities to advance our skills and progress to a new level.

The same is true in an internal leadership practice. Each round of information, practice, dialog, exposure, reflection, understanding, and connecting with others offers us an opportunity to grow a little bit more in understanding and applying our leadership skills.

An internal leadership practice should help us to become self-aware, gather knowledge, and transform into our future self. Remember, we need to learn to be ourselves —with more skill.[1] The goal should be to build a toolbox of knowledge, awareness, and leadership mastery so the tools can be shared with others. Raising our awareness helps us to progress to the next stage of leadership development by updating or replacing our older internal stories.

Ultimately, we consciously or unconsciously decide whether we are willing to engage in this learning process. As we build our internal leadership practice our goal is to increase our consciousness, so we can reflect, choose, and take actions on purpose instead of reacting based on our past experiences, the stories we tell ourselves, and what we have embodied in the past.

As you are developing your internal leadership practice, remember that this practice is the starting point for transformational learning and your evolution to the life you want to live. Leadership development aligns with transformational learning through changes in the stories we tell ourselves. Transformational learning offers us the possibility of lasting transformational change within us as we participate in the process. Transformational learning challenges us to question our internal stories that have been developed by our past experiences and cultural influences, and requires us to inspect each circumstance with a different view. Our internal leadership practice gives us the tools to support this journey.

Supporting Your Internal Leadership Practice

As we are building our internal leadership practice, there are leadership skills we can practice in our jobs, community activities or even our families. The objective is to continue to learn, practice, and refine the necessary interpersonal leadership skills while also working on building a robust internal leadership practice. I think of this as creating a scaffolding for ourselves as we are learning and developing our internal leadership practice. This process can take time.

The term scaffolding comes from both the construction industry and the educational arena. In construction, workmen such as bricklayers and painters put up a scaffold, a temporary platform they can stand or sit on when they are working above the floor; it gives them a relatively safe place to work from when they cannot reach to do their work. The same principle is used in education.

Smaller, more manageable steps are introduced first, and once students have mastered them, they can build on that knowledge and move on to the next phase of their learning.

Scaffolding is essential when we are facing concepts, thoughts, and ideas we have never been exposed to or that challenge to our internal stories. The practice of developing awareness, thoughtful reflection, reflective conversations, and building connections within a community are all needed; and as we learn them, we grow and become more effective leaders.

One of the essential skills is leading without following a script. This is the ability to respond effectively to situations as they happen. The more you learn to lead without a script, the more you master the skill of recognizing what information is missing so it can be obtained and added to the decision-making process. A leader who does not have the right info cannot make good choices.

As a leader, there will be times when you have all the information and there will be times when you don't. Being able to lead without a predetermined script means you understand how to continue to lead even if there is no clear path. There will be times when you will need to be an explorer and forge your own way. There will be times when you will need to connect with and work with your team, advisors and yourself to make the next best move. And when you discover a flaw or an opportunity you will act again.

Leading without a script is having awareness. It is about making meaning of the situation and allows engaging in thoughtful self-reflection and reflective conversations. We develop these skills through our internal leadership practice and our experiences as leaders.

As a person who teaches leadership development, I believe that it could be accomplished in informal ways if we have learned to practice awareness, thoughtful reflection, reflective conversations, and build connections within a community. However, if the focus has been on surviving and/or escaping from blame or undesirable consequences, the chance of people being exposed to and learning to use these essential processes and technique are minimal. It really is essential to build an internal leadership practice.

So, as we aspire to be courageous leaders within our organizations, churches, families, businesses or workplaces, we must provide a scaffold for ourselves as we build our internal leadership practice. We need to become aware of ourselves and our gifts, while recognizing the value of other points of view, and to be willing to learn from concepts and experiences that are unlike our current beliefs. This will help us awaken our consciousness to the possibilities we have missed.

While many areas can influence our internal leadership practice, one thing that is helpful to remember is the concept of "Be." This means *be*coming a leader, someone who consciously practices leadership. It is not just focusing on learning about leadership; it is applying what you learn, doing it, and becoming a leader. West Point Military Academy's leadership model is built on the motto "Be, Know, Do," and it offers insights into leadership development. A leadership practice guides us; it helps us to identify and evaluate what we understand and what we don't, what we could have done differently, how to make effective choices; and it means taking action—doing something.[1]

Remember, being an effective and visible leader is more than what you know or the actions that you take; it is also what you become. This practice of visible leadership, and your internal leadership practice, includes internal work, external influence, and ultimately a connection to a higher purpose, something more significant than you and the community you are a part of.

Informational Learning

Some researchers say, "to be successful, there are certain things leaders must know (knowledge), certain things they must be able to do (skills), and certain ways they must be (character, identity, worldview)."[2]

There are different kinds of learning. The things a leader must know are based on knowledge or informational learning. The things a leader must be able to do can be learned by experience and observational learning. The things a leader must *be* includes their character, which can require a fundamental change within the person.

The growth that involves character and internal change can come through cognitive, spiritual, and identity development. The motto of Know, Do, Be offers a model of how a person learns to be a leader and practices leadership.

When we begin to develop our leadership practice there is a tendency to focus on the knowing and doing. These include the ability to remember facts and execute the advice provided by explicit knowledge. However, a leadership practice also calls for us to become one with ourselves and our sphere of influence.

We need to interrupt our usual way of viewing and interpreting experiences by using tools that encourage us to view experiences through a lens of learning and growth. Practice thoughtful reflection, reflective conversations, and curiosity. Learn to learn from experiences by asking yourself, "What can I learn from this?" or "How could I be wrong about this conclusion?" or "What do I not understand about this situation?" Asking ourselves these questions can start a new way of interpreting issues, interactions, and opportunities, providing us with new ways to view our experiences. Just like a yoga student who practices each week and develops and grows their abilities, you can do the same as a leader.

Thoughtful Reflection
Critical reflection is a tool identified within the transformational learning process that can help your growth.

However, since many people automatically associate the word critical with a negative context, I use the phrase thoughtful reflection instead. Thoughtful reflection is the ability to take an experience and make meaning of it by analyzing and asking questions about what has happened, how and why. Through thoughtful reflection, we identify, assess, and question the assumptions on which our first meaning of the experience was constructed. Thoughtful reflection is taking an in-depth, thoughtful and questioning approach to understanding and thinking about experiences.

Understanding and acknowledging emotions is an essential part of learning and reflection. Reflection, in this context, means thinking deeply about something. Thoughtful reflection is "the ability to challenge our own thoughts, feelings, values, attitudes, beliefs, and habits of mind."[4] Reflection will allow you to develop and practice the ability to take a step outside yourself, and take a look at your part in a situation, while also being present within your experiences. This ability to do both—be part of something and evaluate your role in the situation—at the same time helps us process experiences, understand what is happening from other peoples' points of view too, and to learn from the experience, and not just react to what is happening.

Some researchers tell us that this ability aligns with self-awareness.[6] The strength of self-awareness is that it allows us to look at an experience through a different lens and reshape our interpretation of what happened. It allows us to leave old habits, negativity, and unhelpful ways of thinking and being behind us, and to choose a more positive, abundant view.[5]

Learning to practice reflection helps to strengthen and develop our core selves by gaining new insights into our abilities to influence the changes we desire, to take control of a situation, and to make choices about our future courses of action. Reflection is "the perceptive process by which we change our minds, literally and figuratively. [Reflection] is the process of turning our attention to the justification for what we know, feel, believe and act upon."[7] Reflecting on the outcomes we have observed or experienced may involve the internal practice of new approaches or practices. It requires us to think, consider, and make conscious choices, and not just react because of past experiences or beliefs—especially beliefs we may not even know we have.

Reflection can also uncover our core values, our vision for our future, and our vision of the future we are leading towards.

Often times, I found that when I thought about the phrase core values I was reminded of a paperweight. Something sitting on a shelf in your head, and every once in a while you admire it. So, I had to change the phrase to life filters. Filters seems to be an active concept while values seems passive, to me. When I think about core values as life filters, I think about the filters I use to make decisions, the filters I run daily decisions through.

Each of us must find the life filters that are right for us and for the person or leader we want to be. Ben Franklin is an example of someone who shared his use of values in his life decisions. He identified thirteen virtues he wanted to have as a part of his life, and he used them to govern the type of person he wanted to be.[8] When you have life filters they can help to guide your decisions, because you made a conscious choice about your values and priorities long before the current situation you are facing.

When we reflect on our core values, or life filters, we look to see whether the values we hold are indeed *our* values, they are what we really believe, and they are not just something we have accepted on blind faith or to fit in with the society in which we were raised. We can do this process of taking in-depth thoughtful looks at our values, beliefs, and stories by practicing thoughtful reflection.

One of the exercises I used when I was evaluating my life filters was to answer these questions: How am I going to treat people? How am I going to conduct myself in business? How am I going to treat myself? How am I going to be part of this world? How can I do better? These questions have helped me to determine my life filters and the words I have chosen to be my reminder of how I am going to participate in the world.

Practicing Thoughtful Reflection
Here is a way to start practicing thoughtful reflection, and it's easy. It's called journaling. This is the activity of

writing down and thinking about your experiences, thoughts, and feelings. It helps you to uncover unconscious thoughts and actions. It is also private, and you can do it by making notes on your cell phone or computer, or writing in a notebook. Re-reading what you have written, months later, can give you new insights and understandings that you can bring to new situations.

However, journaling alone will not necessarily lead to thoughtful reflection. It's essential to be able to dig deeper into the thoughts and feelings underneath what you wrote.

I recommend that you use an easy reflection tool when you are just starting out. Borton created a shortlist of questions you ask yourself.[9] It offers a straightforward way to guide your thoughtful reflection. The three simple questions you ask about the experiences and activities you have written about are:

What?

So what?

Now what?

Asking ourselves these questions is often recommended, because they encourage us to analyze what happened, which allows us to learn, instead of focusing on how we felt in that situation.

When I started my personal leadership practice, I

found that asking myself these questions allowed me to take the thoughts and experience from my mind and put them on paper, where I can review them and ask myself questions.

Be able to ask yourself questions that encourage you to practice being curious. Borton's model is one of the most straightforward frameworks I have used to support thoughtful reflection in my personal and professional life. The questions are prompts you can use to aid your reflection. I believe this is the start of building the support scaffold that aspiring leaders need to develop a leadership practice.

Let's look at those three short questions in more detail.

What? This is the description, the start of your self-awareness. All the questions you will ask yourself start with the word what. What happened? What was your reaction? What did you learn? What did you do? What did you expect? What was different? What surprised you? What was the other person thinking? You ask this question to help yourself describe the who, what, why, when, and where.

Next, you move to the question, So what?

So what? So, why does it matter? So, what are the consequences and meanings of your experiences? So, what more do I need to know about this? So, what did I not understand at the time? So, what is the importance of this learning? So, what was different from what I knew previously? So, how do your experiences link to your personal and professional life? So, what emotions, feelings, and actions happened? So, what was the reason you felt that way, or reacted that way? So, what was the reason someone else said, did, or reacted that way?

This helps you to do your analysis and evaluation. It will help you look deeper at what was behind the experience, and why things happened as they did. Then you move to the question, Now what?

Now what? This question helps you to synthesize your understanding, observations and learning. This step helps to build on what we have learned or realized from the previous questions, and it encourages us to consider alternative courses of action and choose what we are going to do next. Now, what are you going to do because of your experiences? Now, what will you do differently? Now, what might be the consequence of taking a particular action? Now, how will you apply what you have learned? Now, what might I do to handle a similar situation better? The Now what part of reflection is essential to our growth as leaders and as people. This will help you start to create your vision of what kind of leader you will be and how you make choices that will impact your life and the lives of other people. What are the key points, the lessons you learned? Are you ready to share them with your family and/or your tribe? How will you do so?

Another thought leader, Byron Katie, teaches different ways of practicing reflection. Byron Katie teaches us to notice, write, question, and turn it around. She teaches us to use excellent questions such as "Is it true? Can you absolutely know that it's true? How do you react, what happens, when you believe that thought?" and "Who would you be without that thought?" This line of questioning allows us to reflect in more depth than you would if you only had the experience and accepted your understanding and interpretation of it at face value.

No matter which method you choose to use, or even if you use both methods, you will benefit. Thoughtful reflection is a "reflection-on-action." It helps us to build a mental reflex that encourages us to question the stories we tell ourselves and believe to be accurate, and not just believe and accept the first impression or feeling we have about an experience.

Reflection-on-action is the process of looking at our past experiences and decisions to gain insights. This is very important as you are working to become a visible leader. We need to be able to challenge our views and thoughts because what we believe may come from faulty or out-of-date internal stories.

Reflection-*in*-action is the next step in thoughtful reflection. It is the ability to reflect or think about what we are doing at the same time as we are performing an action. Donald Schön refers to reflection-in-action by explaining that we take action, and the action itself generates an effect in the situation, and this effect is the feedback we can use to modify, reaffirm, or reframe the method, and continue. This becomes a small internal conversation with the situation through a new way of reacting.

If we think and act this way, what is happening is both an external and an internal change. We are changing the situation as we change our ideas or thoughts at the same time. By the end of the process, we have discovered or created new ways of thinking about the situation. This creates a new mental model for the situation and a whole set of new opinions about what manifested during our action. This process forces our cognitive capacities to evolve. The leadership practice of reflection-in-action is more advanced because it requires reflection at the same time as the activity is occurring.

Reflective Conversations

As you learn to practice thoughtful reflection, the next step is to introduce the concept of reflective conversations. Learn to seek out viewpoints other than your own. This is thoughtful in any leadership practice, and it is a strength for those who practice it often. It helps when we are working to lead other people's understanding, and being aware of all the people affected by our decisions is thoughtful.

Reflective conversations help us to identify and understand who other people are, what interests they have, how they perceive the problem, and how the problem and the solution may affect each of them. Seek clarity about other people's understanding of the situation, opportunity, or challenge; whether it is a technical or social issue, it can open possibilities that thoughtful reflection alone cannot do. Gail K. Boudreaux is President and Chief Executive Officer of Anthem, Inc. In 2018 she won the Billie Jean King Leadership Award. Gail said, "Only when we open our hearts and minds to what's possible...can we achieve all we are destined to become."[10] Gail's quote is exactly right. We need to be able to open our hearts and minds. Reflective conversations are one way to achieve openness.

Using this extended approach, we can include the diverse perspectives of all the people affected by the issue. Understanding this diversity of viewpoints is a requirement for finding good, workable solutions to complex problems. Solving complex problems requires a combination of multiple perspectives, so embracing and being open to the views of other people is thoughtful.

Reflective conversations challenge us to make a thoughtful assessment of our assumptions. This type of reflection requires maturity; we must be aware of and able to control our emotions, and to think clearly about the topic while we are challenging ourselves to consider and work to build a solution. We need to seek out viewpoints that are different from our own.

This process may challenge the frame of reference constructed by your dominant culture. While it is not always possible to reach a consensus, the process of gathering a broad array of views encourages understanding, welcomes differences, and helps to build trust, security, and community.

These conversations are not about winning; they are about practicing open-mindedness. Open-mindedness is a willingness to gather and learn from different perspectives, information and values from people who have different experiences and knowledge to yours. It does not mean losing your commitment to your values. It is the ability to withhold your judgment, listen, and learn.

Reflective conversations are also integral to transformational learning. Transformational learning assists us in challenging the current filters we have used to make meaning of experiences. As we engage in active conversations with other people who have different points of view, we will start to understand their experience and some parts of their internal stories. This is part of our growth as leaders. To develop and grow, it is crucial to "seek out and encourage viewpoints that challenge prevailing norms of the dominant culture in matters of class, race, gender, technology, and environmental protection."[9] Merely going along with others to keep the peace, or to be thought of as "a nice person," is not leadership, and it does not allow us to grow.

When I was seeking out viewpoints that challenged my prevailing norms about women in leadership I found male role models who believe that we need more women in leadership roles. These men understood the potential I had as a leader, and they were willing to invest their time and knowledge in helping me to see my value as a leader, and to learn about leadership. My mentors would have never crossed my path, let alone helped me, if I had stayed where I grew up. No one in my old community could even think about a world where women were equal in leadership. Reflective conversations could not happen in that environment because the community was not emotionally, cognitively, or spiritually open to a different way of being.

Having reflective conversations with viewpoints which challenge your prevailing norms may be easier to say than to do, in the beginning. It takes personal courage to challenge your personal, deeply held beliefs, even if you don't agree with them 100%. Participating in transformational learning, and reflective conversations can be a highly emotional, personal process.

Reflective conversations are about "finding agreement, welcoming differences, 'trying on' other points of view, identifying the common in the contradictory, tolerating anxiety implicitly in paradox, searching for synthesis, and reframing."[11] To participate in reflective conversations, you must be willing to set aside your judgments of what is true or false. Instead, begin by embracing curiosity, and practice being open-minded.

The ability to hold your own opinions while willingly considering other views is essential. It may be a skill you have not mastered or become aware of yet, so it may take some time and practice. And just because you begin a reflective conversation with one opinion does not mean you have to hold onto that opinion. As you learn by hearing other people's information, concerns, and points of view, your opinion may change. Congratulations! You're maturing, and you're growing. It's an essential step to becoming a visible and effective leader.

At the core of reflective conversations is the ability to listen with an open mind and heart. It is also the ability to hold emotions in check even when you don't agree with the other person at all, and to be curious about your own feelings and emotions, as well as theirs. Why do you feel that way, and why do they? Why do you think that way, and why do they? Try to understand their points of view.

This can be tricky to do with people whose cultures have raised them to defend their beliefs without question. But it can be done, especially if you get to practice it multiple times with the same person.

Reflective conversations can be viewed as a mind,

heart, and soul journey. It can be a hard journey full of beauty and sadness, or it can be like a beautiful flower opening, or peeling an onion with many different levels. But learning to have reflective conversations is a necessary art and skill for mastering an authentic internal leadership practice.

The reflective conversation is also a practice you can talk about and model for the emerging leaders you influence through your visible leadership. It sends a powerful message, and is especially needed by leaders today. We need the human connections that come through these conversations. They help us to grow.

Practicing Reflective Conversations

Here are some suggestions for having reflective conversations. Since the environment we are in can influence our emotions and feelings, try to have the conversation in a comfortable neutral environment. A neutral environment will allow the people who are participating in the discussion to feel more equal, and equally valued.

Set simple ground rules for engagement with a reminder to be respectful, and to focus on growth and purpose. Challenge each participant to find and hold onto their inner wisdom, grace, and curiosity while engaging in the conversation.

In the back of my mind, I like to practice reflection-in-action while having in-depth reflective discussions. I try to identify my feelings and emotions—to feel them but not allow them to have influence over me. This can be hard to master.

Having reflective conversations, and finding joy in the knowledge and understanding that is gained from them, can be challenging. There will be times when you may need to ask for a time out to get your emotions back under control.

It is having, or developing, the resilience to keep coming back to reflective conversations and practice that builds mastery. Here are some additional steps you can use to support a reflective conversation.

Once the groundwork has been laid, set your intention to truly understand the other speakers, and listen with your whole self—your ears, eyes, and heart. Listen to the words, the nonverbal cues, the underlying message, and admire the courage the other person needs to have this conversation with you. Ask questions to clarify your understanding. Can you tell me more about...? What was that like?

Affirm your respect for the other person and their effort. You can use statements such as, *I see evidence of* or *you have given this a lot of deep thought*. Then ask questions and invite the other person to make connections and think about future possibilities together. I wonder what would happen if…Who else would be impacted by what we are learning… How has this changed the way you think about…?

By modeling reflective conversations with aspiring leaders, you allow them to verbally reflect and think about experiences.

One of the things I encourage after a reflective conversation is spending time in personal thoughtful reflection and journaling about the conversation. What did you think, feel, and believe before, during, and after the reflective conversation? I find that these thoughtful conversations plant the seeds for more profound growth in the future.

Outside Support for Leadership Practice

Interaction is an essential piece of development and growth within a leadership practice. Parks Daloz said that in her research she "found no instance of transformation as the result of an isolated, epochal event. Indeed, the idea that profound change can occur literally out of the blue flies in the face of everything we know about human development."[12]

Leadership development requires the construction of new meaning structures that help our awareness and our ability to make meaning. Our acquired knowledge, cultural background, psychological makeup, and moral and spiritual beliefs influence how we make meaning from experiences.

Intentionally making meaning cannot happen unless we become aware of our internal stories.

If you are ready to become a visible leader and develop your leadership practice, I encourage you to include mentors, coaches, and communities of practice in your process. Both mentors and coaches can engage in reflective conversations. They can also help by challenging ways of thinking and being that are not productive for aspiring leaders. Challenges are an essential piece of the learning experience. While there is no guarantee that you will learn the lessons from a challenging experience, the support of a person who has an unbiased view can allow and encourage your awareness.

Learning to practice both internal and external awareness helps to heighten our ability to evaluate ourselves and our external experiences. Due to the likelihood of reviewing our experiences through old internal stories which are inadequate, outdated, or biased, and missing potential issues due to our blind spots, we often need to have mentors and coaches who challenge our biases and help with our reflections.

It has been pointed out that although hindsight can be used to protect and serve our view of the situation, it may not be an accurate interpretation because we are viewing it though our personal lens.[13] Intervention may be necessary to help identify our incorrect assumptions. A mentor or coach can help guide your exploration and keep you centered by asking questions you may not ask yourself.

Coaches often are a short-term guide, while mentors are usually a longer-term and a more constant source of guidance for you. Both mentors and coaches can help nurture your thoughtful reflections, offering both opportunities for reflection and challenges while providing support in leadership roles. A mentor or coach can serve as a guide, supporter, challenger, and encourager as we take our developmental journey. As a guide and supporter, a mentor or coach can challenge us to examine our ideas about ourselves and the world, and to formulate new, more developed perspectives. Being supported in our reflections can also encourage us to develop a more profound sense of purpose. Mentoring can also promote our spiritual development and help us to discover a higher purpose.

Another source of outside support for a leadership practice is being involved within communities of practice. Technically, a community of practice is a group of people who share a passion or a concern for something they do, and they regularly interact to learn how to do it better. I have found that I can learn and practice leadership skills by being involved with other people and supporting causes I am passionate about. For example, I learned to be a better communicator and public speaker by joining and attending my local Toastmasters' group. However, I also practiced how to lead meetings and coordinate people serving the group as the local Toastmaster president. We can have learning and practicing opportunities within our everyday activities if we are looking for them and are willing to do the work. We can learn some skills through modeling, not trial and error, and it may speed up the learning process.

Learning within a community allows us to see firsthand what works and what does not. If the environment is both supportive and challenging it offers us an opportunity to practice leadership in a manner that is conducive to leadership development. Communities of practice offer opportunities to learn both the "know that" and the "know how" knowledge. Communities of practice allow us to learn and practice leadership skills and to feel that we belong to a community. Working and learning within a community of practice offers us chances to gain an understanding of tacit knowledge and the opportunity to apply the knowledge we acquire.

Communities of practice also provide an opportunity to learn about the subject and to be a practitioner. The ability to work, connect, and learn within communities of practice offers chances for you to not only "know that" and "know how," but also to *become*. In an active and supportive community of practice, emerging leaders learn about the game (leadership), the rules of engagement, and practice its skills.

Communities of practice also offer an opportunity to build relationships, and to practice building relationships.

Relationships built within an organization influence our awareness and our confidence in our preparation of leadership. According to Parks Daloz, "We develop through relationships, and our sense of self is best understood as a composite of many selves, each constructed out of the intercourse with our evolving worlds."[14] Building relationships with experienced leaders can influence our leadership development within communities of practice.

Putting Practices into Action

When you create a new frame of reference it is important to make opportunities to practice thinking from your fresh perspective. There are learning opportunities everywhere; use your ability to identify, understand, and use chances to makes distinctions between a learning opportunity and a happenstance. The act of realizing that you need to change helps transformational learning; however, it is your ability to put an internal leadership practice into action that brings the real value.

Building an internal leadership practice involves being aware of and embracing the challenges of becoming a leader who is living their amazing life. Learning is "a reflective, dialogical, expressive, and deeply emotional and spiritual self that constructs and re-constructs itself through experiences of learning."[2] You must be open and willing to grow through the development process.

All the parts of the internal leadership practice work

together to help us become more aware of ourselves, of other people, and of the communities you are a part of. The ability to actively look at situations from different viewpoints opens worlds of possibilities and opportunities otherwise missed in the day-to-day busyness of our lives.

Take A Deep Breath and Reflect

What have you already put in place to support your internal leadership practice? What scares you about building an internal leadership practice? What makes you excited?

Take Action

In your reflection journal answer this question: what are you going to commit to, today, to start on this journey? And then take action! Even if it is a small action, take it.

Chapter 11
Barriers and Traps

"If you get stuck, draw with a different pen. Change your tools; it may free your thinking." - Paul Arden

When we are developing an internal leadership practice to support and guide our leadership growth, it is essential to be aware of barriers. Barriers can be emotional, spiritual, cognitive, physical, or any combination of obstacles we experience through our inner dialogue.

Whether these barriers are perceived or real, they are real to us, the person who is experiencing them. These restrictions may be personal beliefs and labels we have assigned to ourselves, or we may have allowed and accepted other people assigning these beliefs and labels to us.

Overcoming our barriers helps us to grow. We need

enough awareness and courage to push through or past them. A barrier can be as simple as needing, for example, to send an application to attend a college and earn a degree you think would help you to be more effective as a leader in your field. The uncertainty of getting accepted, or of being able to go back to school after many years in the workforce, could become a barrier.

There are two choices for engaging with this barrier. You could decide, without even applying, you would not be accepted, and that if you were accepted, you could not achieve this dream. Or, you could choose to fill out the application, which would overcome the first barrier, and do the work it takes to be successful in college after being out of school for so many years, thus defeating the second barrier. Randy Pausch, in his book *The Last Lecture*, talks about these types of obstacles as brick walls.

> The brick walls are there for a reason. The brick walls are not there to keep us out. The brick walls are there to give us a chance to show how badly we want something. Because the brick walls are there to stop the people who don't want it badly enough. They're there to stop the other people.[1]

When we gain the fortitude to view barriers as opportunities to move forward, to get one step closer to living the lives we dream about, we are leading by example.

We may have adopted some barriers due to the people we have allowed into our sphere of influence. If our friends, family, and people we look up to do not see the need for us to undertake leadership growth and development, it will be harder for us to step outside that environment and work on our growth. These may be barriers we experience during our journey to becoming an example of a vibrant, inclusive woman in leadership. Or they may be barriers that emerging leaders who we are trying to help are experiencing.

There are times when another leader can see leadership potential in you, but you do not see those gifts within yourself. If you have not begun to view yourself as a leader, or at least someone who has the potential to lead, you will not respond to opportunities to lead and develop the characteristics of a leader. You might not even be able to see the opportunity because of the filters blocking information you are not actively seeking.

When this barrier comes up we need to seek out people who will encourage us to develop our self-identity as leaders and to help us get over the hurdle. As we discussed in Chapter 6, how we identify ourselves affects our abilities to learn and grow. Even an emerging leader who has tons of potential will never become a great leader if they do not identify themselves as being a leader.

Another barrier can occur when your basic needs are

not met. Participating actively in challenging learning activities and self-growth is difficult, and it is almost impossible when you are just trying to survive. The bottom line is that if our basic needs are not being met, we will not have any additional capacity available to focus on leadership growth and mastery.

When thinking about barriers to our development, it is also essential to understand that adult cognitive development, identity, and spiritual growth are all psychological. Because of their internal nature, there are emotional costs related to each type of development based on the transformation required. Things you once knew for sure may no longer be certain. Indeed, this type of change challenges you not only to change what you know, but also how you know it.

This process can leave you feeling extremely vulnerable, thereby placing personal and professional relationships, loyalties, and the foundations of your life at risk. Beliefs we absorbed without question throughout our lives and our way of viewing the world are no longer adequate for our current situation. Personal strength is required to work through the process of in-depth development due to the challenges related to shaking your core beliefs, worldviews, and internal stories.

Development Traps
In addition to the other barriers we may face as we are trying to become courageous leaders, we can also get

stuck in development traps. These are traps in which we believe we are doing all the right things to get us to our next level, but we are not gaining any traction or making progress. These development traps allow us to deceive ourselves about why we are not growing.

One of my mentors once told me to stop reading books. He said, "I wish you would stop reading so many books and just put into practice something from any one of them. You would be farther ahead." That comment pinched me a little bit. So, I took the advice and filed it in the back part of my brain for future review, and since then I have read or listened to about 400 books and articles (but that is beside the point). As I worked through my research, I began to have a thought circle around in my head. "What if my mentor was right?" What if the very search for knowledge becomes a trap keeping us from growing?

We can get caught in these traps, and then they become loops. Four traps I have identified from my personal experiences are gathering, doing, comparing, and judgment loops. As you read them, you may identify a loop of your own. Each loop has positive and negatives aspects.

But the hardest part of these loops is we may not even realize we are stuck in one. We are doing what we think is the right thing to get the results we want but are not moving forward and really developing as visible leaders.

Gathering information loop: Since you are reading

this book, there is a chance you are stuck in a gathering loop. In this loop, there is an endless search for knowledge. Leaders who are stuck in this loop can be identified by listening to them talk about all the books they read. You read, listen, read, and then read some more. The more you know, the more you want and feel that you need to learn. However, this is where it gets tricky. When do you stop gathering and move into action? How do we break the cycle of gathering and move into the act of doing, and taking actual leadership activities?

Quick questions to ask yourself: How many books have I read this month? How many ideas have I put into practice from what I read? If your ratio of gathering information to taking action is unbalanced, you may need encouragement to move from gathering to taking action.

Becoming aware is the key. My mentor could not make me stop reading books, but he could make a comment to help me start to see that gathering information without taking action was not getting me very far.

Doing loop: While it may seem that taking action is a good thing, this loop may be even more dangerous than the gathering loop; because when you are caught up in an action loop, you think that you are accomplishing something because you are busy. This could happen as a reaction to becoming aware of the gathering loop, or it could be your natural way of being. Because of this awareness, you may decide you are not going to read another book, ever, and you are only going to take action. Unlike the gathering loop, which is always seeking information but never doing much (or anything) with the information you have gathered, the doing loop is about being busy. But the busyness never gets more in-depth or very focused because there is no prioritization, no vision or goal. If you never challenge yourself or seek information to help you see things differently, you could be very busy but accomplish nothing.

Quick questions to ask yourself: When was the last time I read or listened to someone with more knowledge about the areas of leadership I'm working on, or need to work on? When was the last time I invested in my self-development? What am I focused on right now?

If the questions are hard to answer, you may be stuck in the doing loop.

Comparing loop: This loop can be hard to break. When you are have decided to become a visible leader, there is a tendency to look at other leaders who are farther along in their journey and compare yourself to them. If it's not handled appropriately, comparing yourself to others can do more harm than good, because the comparison can become an unattainable vision of who you believe you should be and the skills you think you should already have mastered.

While there are dangers in this loop, there are also benefits. The ability to understand how experienced leaders behave, treat others, and lead, can help you design your journey. Just remind yourself that you are a work in progress, and keep moving toward becoming more of yourself—with more skills.

Questions to ask yourself: What am I doing to grow as a leader? How have I changed and grown in the past year? What have I done to inspire others to develop and grow?

If you answer the questions by brushing off your contributions and then go right into what another leader is doing better, you could be stuck in this loop. Each of us must learn to love and appreciate who we are and what we offer the world.

Judgement Loop: As I became more self-aware, I realized that I was not kind to myself. I would never in a million years say the things I was saying to myself to another person, but I was mentally saying them to myself. For a while I was stuck in the judgment loop, and I had to break this vicious cycle and decide to become my biggest fan and supporter.

It took time and effort, and there are still times when I have to remind myself that I will succeed or fail based on what I believe and what I am telling myself. I have to catch myself when I'm not being mentally supportive of my initiatives and correct myself. It is a practice requiring discipline on my part, every day. But the payoff that I have found from becoming my biggest supporter and fan is more than I would ever have dreamed.

Ask yourself questions about how you see yourself and how you feel about yourself. If you are stuck in this loop you are harming yourself more then you realize. You are also hurting other people who are looking at you as a role model. This judgment loop affects your leader self-identity, which can be fragile when you are just starting out. You can find others who will offer you positive reinforcement, but it is up to you to become your own biggest fan a and supporter.

There is a loop or a cycle each of us goes through in every area of our lives. We are born, grow, die. However, somewhere in our growing and development phase, we can get caught in a loop of some type. The loop started as a good thing but eventually it will keep you from reaching your full potential. These barriers and traps are the very reason we need to create an internal leadership practice. Your ability to reflect, have meaningful conversations, and be involved in a community can allow you to recognize when something is keeping you from achieving your full potential.

Take A Deep Breath and Reflect

What loop are you in? Where do you need to take action, to learn more, to love yourself just the way you are? How have you been holding yourself back from being the leader you are called to be? If someone else came to you with the same problem, what advice would you give them to break out of their loop?

Take Action

In your reflection journal make a note about what barriers or loops you may be stuck in. If you are not sure, ask yourself to pay attention to what you feel called to do and what is keeping you from taking real action.

Chapter 12
Circle of Influence

"Our character is mainly shaped by our primary social community - the people with whom we eat, play, converse, and study."- Timothy Keller

T he work of a leader is helping others to grow. Building your leadership skills, internal leadership practice and engaging with communities, mentors, and coaches are essential in our development as leaders. But as you engage in visible leadership, you need to also become a contributing member of these communities.

Leadership is not always about us and our development. It cannot be, because at its core it is influence between the environment, followers and leaders.

There comes a point in our personal leadership growth when leadership needs to become focused on what you can do for others, including the people who are behind you on your leadership journey. Who are you helping after you have put your mask on and are breathing well? Who are you investing in, and how are the people you are leading—are they gaining confidence, growing and developing?

I believe the starfish story by Loren Eisley is a perfect example of why we need to focus on our circle of influence.

One day a man was walking along the beach when he noticed a boy picking something up and gently throwing it into the ocean. Approaching the boy, he asked, "What are you doing?" The youth replied, "Throwing starfish back into the ocean. The surf is up and the tide is going out. If I don't throw them back, they'll die." "Son," the man said, "don't you realize there are miles and miles of beach and hundreds of starfish? You can't make a difference!"

After listening politely, the boy bent down, picked up another starfish, and threw it back into the surf. Then, smiling at the man, he said, "I made a difference for that one."

We can make a difference to one person. Perhaps your niece is struggling in high school and you tutor her in math. Or your local homeless shelter may need help with fundraising so they can continue their services. Your circle of influence may be your immediate family and friends, or it may be the people you interact with at work and at the gym. Or perhaps you will become a superstar who is well known in the world and influence the lives of thousands of people. Each of us has people who we are interacting with, and we are influencing their lives.

As leaders, we can get caught up and look around, thinking that our impact is not significant enough. But if we remember the starfish story and focus on making a difference for one person, one family, one community, one state, one country, one world, we make an essential impact on another human being.

Often, we can get caught, like I was in the diversity exercise. We can become so focused on ourselves and where we want to be that we don't see all the people we have walked past on our way to our success. This giving back should happen sooner rather than later; and you do not need to feel 100% confident about your abilities. You are already ahead of someone else on their journey. The example you are sharing will be just right for them.

I decided to intentionally to keep my focus on making a difference for others on their journey. One practice I am intentional about doing is to teach what I learn. So, I share what I am learning with leaders who are still growing, and also with leaders who I think are ahead of me on their journey. In both situations, I try to ask really thoughtful questions and share what I have experienced. I have found aspiring leaders and built relationships with them. My focus is not to change the world but to make a difference in one person's life. I wrote this book for you, to make an impact on your leadership and your life.

Stepping out and making a conscious effort to make a difference in another person's life, career and development can be intimidating. If you are not confident enough to share with people you think are ahead of you, share what you are learning with aspiring leaders. Have coffee together and discuss what you are reading, what you have experienced, what you are learning. Reach out to aspiring leaders, and remember that if we take a moment and pour our learning and encouragement into them, as we wished others had done for us, we could make a significant impact on the future of leaders in our organizations and our lives.

Building a leadership practice focuses on our internal development. This practice sets the scaffold in place to support all our future learning, engagement, and transformation. Without an internal leadership practice of thoughtful reflection, reflective conversations and outside support, you may learn leadership skills; but you may not develop the core inner strength of self-awareness, and other strengths you will need to move to your next levels in cognitive, spiritual or identity development.

Take A Deep Breath and Reflect

Who is your starfish? The one person, family, or community that you need to be intentional about interacting with and influencing?

Take Action

In your reflection journal answer this question: what are you going do right now to make sure you are connecting and supporting that one person? Make a commitment right now, then call them, email them, or do what you need to do to start the process. Do not wait!

Chapter 13
Conclusion

"Sunsets are proof that endings can often be beautiful too."
— Beau Taplin

The beauty of becoming a visible leader is that when emerging leaders are looking for an example to model their leadership after they can find examples of both male and female leaders. These leaders can embody being trustworthy, dependable, adaptable, helpful, creative, sincere, cooperative, friendly, empathetic, encouraging, patient, understanding, self-motivated, considerate, and effective problem-solvers. And as you start to make a positive mark on another person's life map, you are truly becoming the leader you were created to be—a woman who loves herself enough to embrace her journey and lead others to embrace theirs.

Here is what I know for sure: the WORLD needs YOU to LEAD. Leadership is not about being the boss, being the top person, being the one calling the shots. It's about being the woman who is willing to be strong, confident, and ready to take chances, a woman who loves all of herself enough to lead and enough to allow others the space to be amazing as well. We set the stage for the next generations of leaders, by how we conduct ourselves.

The biggest challenge is being willing to take an uncertain step into the area where you have been called to lead and START making an impact. Stop waiting for it to be the right time, the right community, the right person, and make a difference right now.

I had to decide to let my light shine—without worrying whether it was perfect, and without worrying about whether I was doing it right—because I had made a choice to make a DIFFERENCE to individuals who are trying to become leaders, individuals who want to help their teams grow so they can make an impact together, who want to lead within their families and their communities.

I found a quote that spoke to me as I was trying to become a better version of myself both personally and professionally. I have shared it in almost all of my books as it inspires me so much. I hope it will inspire you as well. It comes from *Our Deepest Fear* by Marianne Williamson.

Our deepest fear is not that we are inadequate. Our deepest fear is that we are powerful beyond measure. It is our light, not our darkness that most frightens us. We ask ourselves, 'Who am I to be brilliant, gorgeous, talented, fabulous?'

Actually, who are you not to be? You are a child of God. Your playing small does not serve the world. There is nothing enlightened about shrinking so that other people won't feel insecure around you. We are all meant to shine, as children do. We were born to make manifest the glory of God that is within us. It's not just in some of us; it's in everyone. And as we let our own light shine, we unconsciously give other people permission to do the same. As we are liberated from our own fear, our presence automatically liberates others.

Those last two lines called me to take a stand. We NEED leaders, leaders who embrace their whole selves, leaders who let their light shine and encourage others to do the same.

I am on a mission to inspire women who want to live amazing lives, full of accomplished dreams, and who influence others to do the same—women who know they have to find their personal visions for their lives and to find the courage to bring that life into reality.

It always begins inside of us; within the internal stories we tell ourselves. If we cannot help ourselves, we cannot help others. If we cannot lead ourselves, it is harder to guide others. If we cannot love ourselves because of our flaws as well as our amazingness, we miss the opportunity to love others and to help them love themselves.

If we are aware of ourselves, our invisible roots, and the stories we tell ourselves we can choose which voice to keep in our internal dialogues and which voice to stop hearing.

Be willing to do the work it takes to build your own internal leadership practice. The ability to understand and accept yourself can be one of the hardest and most rewarding parts of your journey. The more you choose to be your own biggest fan and supporter, the faster you can take action.

The more you build community and find your tribes of people who support you, and who you support, the more opportunities you will have. We cannot grow and develop into the leaders we are meant to be without other people in our lives. We need these connections to see the possibilities, to learn and to practice. We need to choose with care the people we allow to have influence in our lives. And we need to make our leadership visible to the aspiring leaders who are a couple of steps behind us so we can help them reach their full potential.

Take A Deep Breath and The Final Reflection

What do I need to do as a result of what I have learned and what I have thought about in this book? What questions can I ask myself that I have avoided asking so far, or what I have I not thought about? Who do I need to have conversations with? Who should I be building community with? Who is behind me on this journey, and I could have coffee with them and encourage their growth? Who should I loan this book to? And what has changed in my understanding of leadership and becoming a leader? What has changed in the way I interact with other people as a leader?

Take Action

In your reflection journal answer this question: What I am committed to doing right now to continue my leadership journey? If you are not doing anything right now, what do you think you should be doing, and when are you going to start? Who can you ask for advice that may point you in the right direction? Ask yourself, what do I have to take action on in the next month, in three months, next year and the next five years?

Spend some time thinking about these questions and writing about them. Also, write about any concerns you have, any obstacles you think you will encounter, who you can turn to for advice, encouragement, information—and what action you can take.

Note: Your plans may change, and your life and seasons will change; but if you have a plan and you are willing to be flexible you will continue moving toward becoming the leader you feel called to be.

Additional Resources & Endnotes

Chapter 1

1 Marillyn Hewson Interview with CBS https://www.cbsnews.com/news/marillyn-hewson-lockheed-martins-first-female-ceo-on-running-worlds-largest-defense-contractor/

2 Marissa Mayer, https://www.britannica.com/biography/Marissa-Mayer https://www.inc.com/john-brandon/20-marissa-mayer-quotes-on-making-smart-business-choices.html

Chapter 2

1 Andreas, S. (2016). *Career advancement strategies for emerging leaders: Get promoted faster in the career you love.* Strasburg, Oh: WiseWood, LLC

Chapter 3

1 Mary Barra https://www.industryweek.com/companies-amp-executives/did-mary-barra-s-inclusive-leadership-style-propel-her-top and https://www.latimes.com/business/autos/la-fi-hy-mary-barra-gm-ceo-20131211-story.html#axzz2rAIzEROr

Goffee, R. & Jones G. (2015). Why should anyone be led by you? Pg. 85. Boston, MA: Harvard Business School Publishing.

Liming, Z., Majid, S., Raihana, S., & Tong, S. (2012). Importance of soft skills for education and career success. *International Journal for Cross-Disciplinary Subjects in Education*, 2, 1036-1042. doi:10.20533/ijcdse.2042.6364.2012.0147

Mitchell, G. W., Skinner, L. B., & White, B. J. (2010). Essential soft skills for success in the twenty-first century workforce as perceived by business educators. *Delta Pi Epsilon Journal*, 52, 43-53. Retrieved from https://www.learntechlib.org/j/ISSN-0011-8052/

Chapter 4

1 Taylor, K. (2000). Teaching with developmental intention. In J. Mezirow & Associates (Eds.), *Learning as transformation: Critical perspectives on a theory in progress* (pp. 151-180, p. 162). San Francisco, CA: Jossey-Bass.

2 Kegan, R., & Lahey, L. (2009). *Immunity to change: How to overcome it and unlock potential in yourself and your organization.* Boston, MA: Harvard Business School Press.

Dirkx, J. M. (1998). Transformative learning theory in the practice of adult education: An overview. *PAACE Journal of Lifelong Learning*, 7, 1-14. Retrieved from https://link.springer.com/chapter/10.1007/978-94-6300-797-9_2

Hiebert, P. (2008*). Transforming worldviews: An anthropological understanding of how people change.* Grand Rapids, MI: Baker Academic.

Kegan, R. (2000). What "form" transforms? A constructive-development approach to transformational learning. In J. Mezirow & Associates (Eds.), *Learning as transformation: Critical perspectives on a theory in progress* (pp. 35-70, p.67). San Francisco, CA: Jossey-Bass.

Mezirow, J. (2000). Learning to think like an adult: Core concepts of transformational learning. In J. Mezirow & Associates (Eds.), *Learning as transformation: Critical perspectives on a theory in progress* (pp. 3-34). San Francisco, CA: Jossey-Bass.

Chapter 5

1 Strozzi-Heckler, R. (2014). The art of somatic coaching. p. 14. North Atlantic Books: Berkeley, CA.

2 Maltz, M. (2015). Psycho-Cybernetics: Updated and expanded. p. prefix New York, NY: Perigee

Amy Cuddy
https://www.ted.com/talks/amy_cuddy_your_body_language_shapes_who_you_are?language=en

Malik, A. (2012). Perfection – The right perspective. *Hilal*, 49(5).

Rhoda Troyer http://rigandco.com/

Chapter 6

1 Duguid, P. (2007). "The art of knowing": Social and tacit dimensions of knowledge and the limits of the community of practice, *The Information Society*, 21, 109-118. doi:10.1080/01972240590925311

2 Abigail Johnson https://www.glassdoor.com/blog/fidelity-ceo-abby-johnson/

3 Marillyn Hewson https://www.cbsnews.com/news/marillyn-hewson-lockheed-martins-first-female-ceo-on-running-worlds-largest-defense-contractor/

4 Ginni Rometty https://www.cnbc.com/2017/06/21/what-ibm-ceo-ginni-rometty-

learned-from-her-mom-when-her-dad-left.html

5 Bolden, R., Gosling, J., Hawkins, B., & Taylor, S. (2011). *Exploring leadership*. Pg. 39. Oxford, England: Oxford University Press.

Fadjukoff, P., Kokko, K., & Pulkkinen, L. (2007). Implications of timing of entering adulthood for identity achievement. *Journal of Adolescent Research*, 22, 504-530. doi:10.1177/0743558407305420

Hall, R. J., & Lord, R. G. (2005). Identity, deep structure and the development of leadership skill. *The Leadership Quarterly*, 16, 591-615. doi:10.1016/j.leaqua.2005.06.003

Howard, J. A. (2000). Social psychology of identities. *Annual Review of Sociology*, 26, 367-393. doi:0360-0572/00/0815-0367

Kegan, R. (2000). What "form" transforms? A constructive-development approach to transformational learning. In J. Mezirow & Associates (Eds.), *Learning as transformation: Critical perspectives on a theory in progress* (pp. 35-70, p.67). San Francisco, CA: Jossey-Bass.

Kegan, R., & Lahey, L. (2009*). Immunity to change: How to overcome it and unlock potential in yourself and your organization.* Boston, MA: Harvard Business School Press.

Kim, S., & Merriam, S. B. (2012). Studying transformative learning: What methodology. In P. Cranton & E. W. Taylor (Eds.), *The handbook of transformative learning: Theory, research, and practice* (pp. 56-72). San Francisco, CA: Jossey-Bass.

Komives, S. R., Longerbeam, S. D., Mainella, F. C. & Osteen, L., & Owen, J. E. (2005). Developing a leadership identity: A grounded theory. *Journal of College Student Development*, 46, 593-611. doi:10.1353/csd.2005.0061

Komives, S. R., Longerbeam, S. D., Mainella, F. C., Osteen, L., & Owen, J. E. (2006). A leadership identity development model: Applications from a grounded theory. *Journal of College Student Development*, 47, 401-418. doi:10.1353/csd.2006.0048

Mezirow, J. (2000). Learning to think like an adult: Core concepts of transformational learning. In J. Mezirow & Associates (Eds.), *Learning as transformation: Critical perspectives on a theory in progress* (pp. 3-34). San Francisco, CA: Jossey-Bass.

Montero, R., Quintana, S. M., & Scull, N. C., (2008). Identity development. In F. T. L. Leong, E. M. Altmaier, & B. D. Johnson (Eds.), *Encyclopedia of counseling* (Vol. 3, pp. 1163-1168). Thousand Oaks, CA: Sage.

Parks Daloz, L. (2000). Transformative learning for the common good. In J. Mezirow & Associates (Eds.), *Learning as transformation: Critical perspectives on a theory in progress* (pp. 103-124). San Francisco, CA: Jossey-Bass.

Ritzer, G., & Stepnisky, J. (2014). *Sociological theory* (9th ed.). New York, NY: McGraw-Hill.

Chapter 7

1 Malik, A. (2012). Perfection – The right perspective. *Hilal*, 49(5).

2 Tisdell, E., & Tolliver, D. (2006). Engaging spirituality in the transformative higher education classroom. *New Directions for Adult and Continuing Education*, 2006(109), 37-47. doi:10.1002/ace.206

3 Lauzon, A. C. (2013). A reflection on an emergent spirituality and the practice of adult education. *Canadian Journal of University Continuing Education*, 33(2), 35-48. Pg.42. doi:10.21225/D5N88S [1]

Brookfield, S. (2000). Transformative learning as ideology critique. In J. Mezirow & Associates (Eds.), Learning as transformation: Critical perspectives on a theory in progress (pp. 125-148). San Francisco, CA: Jossey-Bass.

Cranton, P., & Taylor, E. W. (2012). Transformative learning theory: Seeking a more unified theory. In P. Cranton & E. W. Taylor (Eds.), The handbook of transformative learning: Theory, research, and practice (pp. 3-20). San Francisco, CA: Jossey-Bass.

Kinjerski, V. M., & Skrypnek, B. J. (2004). Defining spirit at work: Finding common ground. *Journal of Organizational Change Management*, 17, 26-42. doi:10.1108/09534810410511288

Roof, R. A. (2015). The association of individual spirituality on employee engagement: *The spirit at work. Journal of Business Ethics*, 130, 585-599. doi:10.1007/s10551-014-2246-0

Wilber, K. (2000). *Integral psychology: Consciousness, spirit, psychology, therapy*. Boston, MA: Shambhala.

Chapter 8

1 Hobbs, J. (2014). The short and tragic life of Robert Peace: A brilliant young man who left Newark for the Ivy League. New York, NY: Scribner

2 Baumgartner, K. M. (2001). An update on transformational learning. New Directions for Adult and Continuing Education, 89, 15-24. Pg. 19. doi:10.1002/ace.4

3 Taylor, K. (2000). Teaching with developmental intention. In J. Mezirow & Associates (Eds.), *Learning as transformation: Critical perspectives on a theory in progress* (pp. 151-180, p. 155). San Francisco, CA: Jossey-Bass.

4 Mezirow, J. (2000). Learning to think like an adult: Core concepts of transformational learning. In J. Mezirow & Associates (Eds.), *Learning as transformation: Critical perspectives on a theory in progress* (pp. 3-34, quote p. 82). San Francisco, CA: Jossey-Bass.

Baumgartner, L., Caffarella, R., & Merriam, S. (2007). Learning in adulthood: A comprehensive guide. Hoboken, NJ: Wiley.

Bierema, L., & Merriam, S. B. (2014). *Adult learning: Linking theory and practice.* San Francisco, CA: Jossey-Bass.

Fisher, J. (2011). The four domains model: Connecting spirituality, health and well-being. *Religions*, 2(1), 17-28. doi:10.3390/rel2010017

Kegan, R. (2000). What "form" transforms? A constructive-development approach to transformational learning. In J. Mezirow & Associates (Eds.), *Learning as transformation: Critical perspectives on a theory in progress* (pp. 35-70). San Francisco, CA: Jossey-Bass.

MacKeracher, D. (2012). The role of experience in transformative learning. In P. Cranton & E. W. Taylor (Eds.), *The handbook of transformative learning: Theory, research, and practice* (pp. 342-354). San Francisco, CA: Jossey-Bass.

McCall, M. W., Jr. (2010). Recasting leadership development. *Industrial and Organizational Psychology*, 3, 3-19. doi:10.1111/j.1754-9434.2009.01189.x

Chapter 9

1 George, B. (2007). *Discover your true north*. Pg. 89. Hoboken, NJ: John Wiley & Sons, Inc.

2 Jim Rohn quote, https://www.businessinsider.com/jim-rohn-youre-the-average-

of-the-five-people-you-spend-the-most-time-with-2012-7

3 Kets de Vries, M. F. R., & Korotov, K. (2012). Transformation leadership development programs: Creating long-term sustainable change. In R. Khurana, N. Nohria, & S. Snook (Eds.*),* *The handbook for teaching leadership: Knowing, doing and being* (pp. 263-282, quote p.268). Thousand Oaks, CA: Sage.

Bandura, A. (2001). Social cognitive theory: An agentic perspective. *Annual Review of Psychology,* 52, 1-26. doi:10.1146/annurev.psych.52.1.1

Burke, H., & Mancuso, L. (2012). Social cognitive theory, metacognition, and simulation learning in nursing education. *Journal of Nursing Education,* 51, 543-548. doi:10.3928/01484834-20120820-02

Goffee, R. & Jones, G. (2015). *Why should anyone be led by you: What it takes to be an authentic leader. P. 82.* Boston, MA: Harvard Business School Publishing

Marsick, V. J., & Watkins, K. E. (2001). Informal and incidental learning. *New Directions for Adult and Continuing Education,* 2001(89), 25-34. doi:10.1002/ace.5

Mezirow, J. (2000). Learning to think like an adult: Core concepts of transformational learning. In J. Mezirow & Associates (Eds.), *Learning as transformation: Critical perspectives on a theory in progress* (pp. 3-34). San Francisco, CA: Jossey-Bass.

Taylor, K. (2000). Teaching with developmental intention. In J. Mezirow & Associates (Eds.), *Learning as transformation: Critical perspectives on a theory in progress* (pp. 151-180). San Francisco, CA: Jossey-Bass.

Vygotsky, L. S. (1978). Interaction between learning and development (M. Lopez-Morillas, Trans.). In M. Cole, V. John-Steiner, S. Scribner, & E. Souberman (Eds.), *Mind in society: The development of higher psychological processes* (pp. 79-91). Cambridge, MA: Harvard University Press.

Chapter 10

1 Goffee, R. & Jones G. (2015). *Why should anyone be led by you? Pg. 85* Boston, MA: Harvard Business School Publishing.

2 Khurana, R., Nohria, N., & Snook, S. (2012). Teaching leadership: Advancing the field. In R. Khurana, N. Nohria, & S. Snook (Eds.), *The handbook for teaching leadership: Knowing, doing and being* (pp. xi-xxix, quote p. xv). Thousand Oaks,

CA: Sage.

3 Snook, S. (2004). Be, know, do: Forming character the West Point way. *Compass*, 1(2), 16-19. Retrieved from http://www.hbs.edu/faculty/Pages/item.aspx?num=31780

4/5 Hall, C., & Starkey, K. (2012). The spirit of leadership: New directions in leadership education. In R. Khurana, N. Nohria, & S. Snook (Eds.), *The handbook for teaching leadership: Knowing, doing and being* (pp. 81-98, quote on p. 89, **90**). Thousand Oaks, CA: Sage.

6 Jasper, M (2003). *Beginning reflective practice.* Cheltenham: Nelson Thornes.

7 Mezirow, J. (1991). *Transformative dimensions of adult learning.* p. 46. San Francisco, CA: Jossey-Bass.

8 Ben Franklin autobiography http://www.ushistory.org/franklin/autobiography/page38.htm

9 Queen Mary University of London. Guidance on Reflective Writing. http://qmplus.qmul.ac.uk/mod/book/view.php?id=257889 [acces sed 15 June 2017] and Borton's Development Framework. https://www.physio-pedia.com/index.php?title=Borton%27s_Development_Framework&oldid =146680

10 Gail K Boudreaux Interview https://www.womenssportsfoundation.org/programs/awards/2018-billie-jean-king-leadership-award-gail-k-boudreaux/

11 Mezirow, J. (1997). Transformative learning: Theory to practice. *New Directions for Adult and Continuing Education*, 1997(74), 5-12. doi:10.1002/ace.7401

12 Mezirow, J. (2000). Learning to think like an adult: Core concepts of transformational learning. In J. Mezirow & Associates (Eds.), *Learning as transformation: Critical perspectives on a theory in progress* (pp. 3-34, quote p.13). San Francisco, CA: Jossey-Bass, 2000).

11-13 Parks Daloz, L. (2000). Transformative learning for the common good. In J. Mezirow & Associates (Eds.), *Learning as transformation: Critical perspectives on a theory in progress* (pp. 103-124, quote p.106/115). San Francisco, CA: Jossey-Bass.

14 Freeman, M. P. (2010). *Hindsight: The promise and peril of looking backward. (p.7)* Oxford, England: Oxford University Press.

Bandura, A. (1977). *Social learning theory.* Englewood Cliffs, NJ: Prentice-Hall.

Baumgartner, K. M. (2001). An update on transformational learning. *New Directions for Adult and Continuing Education, 89,* 15-24. doi:10.1002/ace.4

Baumgartner, L., Caffarella, R., & Merriam, S. (2007). *Learning in adulthood: A comprehensive guide.* San Francisco, CA: Jossey-Bass.

Belenky, M., & Stanton, A. (2000). Inequality, development and connected knowing. In J. Mezirow, J. & Associates (Eds.), *Learning as transformation: Critical perspectives on a theory in progress* (pp. 71-102). San Francisco, CA: Jossey-Bass.

Bonk, C. J., & Kim, K. A. (1998). Extending sociocultural theory to adult learning. In M. C. Smith & T. Pourchot (Ed.), *Adult learning and development: Perspectives from educational psychology* (pp. 67-88). New York, NY: Lawrence Erlbaum.

Brookfield, S. (2000). Transformative learning as ideology critique. In J. Mezirow & Associates (Eds.), *Learning as transformation: Critical perspectives on a theory in progress* (pp. 125-148). San Francisco, CA: Jossey-Bass.

Cranton, P. (2000). Individual difference and transformative learning. In J. Mezirow & Associates (Eds.), Learning as transformation: Critical perspectives on a theory in progress (pp. 181-204). San Francisco, CA: Jossey-Bass.

Cranton, P., & Taylor, E. W. (2012). Transformative learning theory: Seeking a more unified theory. In P. Cranton & E. W. Taylor (Eds.), *The handbook of transformative learning: Theory, research, and practice* (pp. 3-20). San Francisco, CA: Jossey-Bass.

Csoka, L. S. (2012). Being a leader: Mental strength for leadership. In R. Khurana, N. Nohria, & S. Snook (Eds.), *The handbook for teaching leadership: Knowing, doing and being* (pp. 213-226). Thousand Oaks, CA: Sage.

Day, D. V., Halpin, S., & Harrison, M. M. (2009). *An integrative approach to leader development: Connecting adult development, identity, and expertise.* New York, NY: Routledge.

Duguid, Paul. (2007). "The art of knowing": Social and tacit dimensions of knowledge and the limits of the community of practice, *The Information Society,* 21, 109-118. doi:10.1080/01972240590925311Kim & Merriam,

2012).

Elias, D., & Kasl, E. (2000). Creating new habits of mind in small groups. In J. Mezirow & Associates (Eds.), *Learning as transformation: Critical perspectives on a theory in progress* (pp. 229-252). San Francisco, CA: Jossey-Bass.

Fisher, J. (2011). The four domains model: Connecting spirituality, health and well-being. *Religions*, 2(1), 17-28. doi:10.3390/rel2010017

George, B. (2007). *Discover your true north. P.82* Hoboken, NJ: John Wiley & Sons, Inc.

Hall, R. J., & Lord, R. G. (2005). Identity, deep structure and the development of leadership skill. *The Leadership Quarterly*, 16, 591-615. doi:10.1016/j.leaqua.2005.06.003

Hansman, C. (2001). Context-based adult learning. *New Directions for Adult & Continuing Education*, 2001(89), 43-52. doi:10.1002/ace.7

Komives, S. R., Longerbeam, S. D., Mainella, F. C. & Osteen, L., & Owen, J. E. (2005). Developing a leadership identity: A grounded theory. *Journal of College Student Development*, 46, 593-611. doi:10.1353/csd.2005.0061

Kraiger, K., Salas, E., Smith-Jentsch, K. A., & Tannenbaum, S. I. (2012). The science of training and development in organizations: What matters in practice. *Psychological Science in the Public Interest*, 13, 74-101. doi:10.1177/1529100612436661

Lauzon, A. C. (2013). A reflection on an emergent spirituality and the practice of adult education. *Canadian Journal of University Continuing Education*, 33(2), 35-48. doi:10.21225/D5N88S

MacKeracher, D. (2012). The role of experience in transformative learning. In P. Cranton & E. W. Taylor (Eds.), *The handbook of transformative learning: Theory, research, and practice* (pp. 342-354). San Francisco, CA: Jossey-Bass.

Malik, M. (2016). Assessment of a professional development program on adult learning theory. *Libraries and the Academy*, 16, 47-70. doi:10.1353/pla.2016.0007

Maltz, M. (2002). *The new psycho-cybernetics*. New York, NY: Prentice Hall Press.

Marsick, V. J., & Watkins, K. E. (2001). Informal and incidental learning. *New Directions for Adult and Continuing Education*, 2001(89), 25-34.

doi:10.1002/ace.5McCall, 2010).

Schön, Donald. 1983 *The Reflective Practitioner*, Basic Books Inc.

Tisdell, E., & Tolliver, D. (2006). Engaging spirituality in the transformative higher education classroom. *New Directions for Adult and Continuing Education*, 2006(109), 37-47. doi:10.1002/ace.206

Chapter 11
1 Pausch, R. (2008) *The last lecture. (p. 79)* New York, NY: Hyperionn

Kegan, R. (2000). What "form" transforms? A constructive-development approach to transformational learning. In J. Mezirow & Associates (Eds.), *Learning as transformation: Critical perspectives on a theory in progress* (pp. 35-70). San Francisco, CA: Jossey-Bass.

Komives, S. R., Longerbeam, S. D., Mainella, F. C. & Osteen, L., & Owen, J. E. (2005). Developing a leadership identity: A grounded theory. *Journal of College Student Development*, 46, 593-611. doi:10.1353/csd.2005.0061

Taylor, K. (2000). Teaching with developmental intention. In J. Mezirow & Associates (Eds.), *Learning as transformation: Critical perspectives on a theory in progress* (pp. 151-180). San Francisco, CA: Jossey-Bass.

Chapter 12
1 Eiseley, L. (1978). The star thrower. p.19. New York, NY: Times Books

2 Dirkx, J. M. (1998). Transformative learning theory in the practice of adult education: An overview. *PAACE Journal of Lifelong Learning*, 7, 1-14. Quote p.10. Retrieved from http://www.dlc.riversideinnovationcentre.co.uk/wp-content/uploads/2012/10/Transformative-Learning-in-Adult-Education-Dirkx-19981.pdf

Chapter 13

Williamson, M. (1996). *A Return To Love: Reflections on the Principles of A Course in Miracles*. New York, NY: HarperOne

About the Author

Dr. Sarah Andreas is an author, speaker and leadership coach who has helped amazing individuals transform their personal and professional lives via her workshops, private sessions, public appearances, articles, products, and books. As the founder of WiseWood LLC, her purpose in life is to teach, research, coach and write about leadership development with a specific focus on helping individuals live and lead lives they love.

Sarah has earned a Master of Business Administration degree from Malone University and a Ph.D. in Organizational Leadership from Johnson University. Her love for business, people and leadership gives her a unique perspective on leadership development and helping people to achieve their fullest potential.

www.ingramcontent.com/pod-product-compliance
Lightning Source LLC
Chambersburg PA
CBHW021332090426
42742CB00008B/576